CIGARETTE
PACK ART

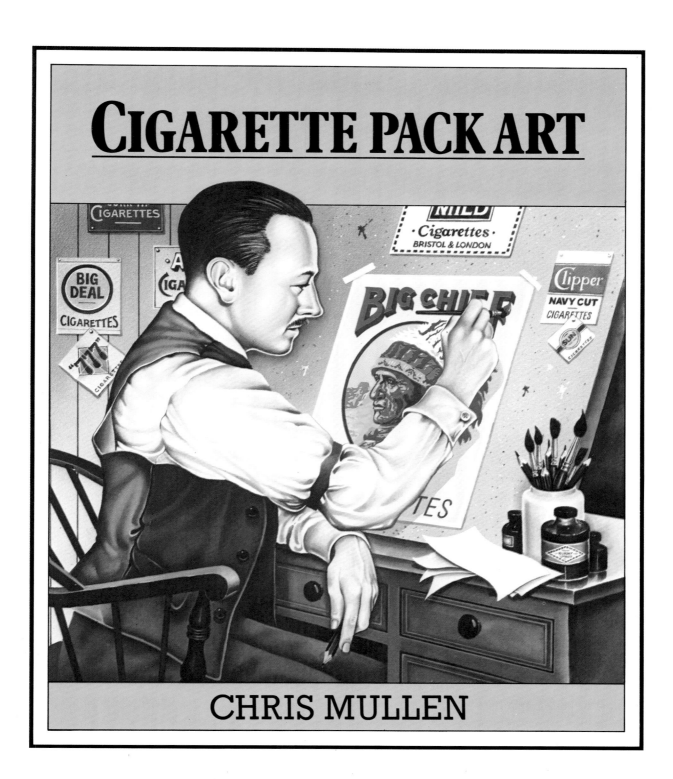

CIGARETTE PACK ART

CHRIS MULLEN

HAMLYN
London · New York · Sydney · Toronto

ACKNOWLEDGEMENTS

The author and publishers gratefully acknowledge the invaluable help of all those who have contributed to the compilation of this book. They would particularly like to thank the following:

Pack collectors in Britain and the USA, who so generously allowed access to their collections for photography and helped with information, research and dating: Alan Barker, Nat Chait, Hilary Humphries in Britain; Richard Elliott, Roger Hordines, Jerry Mackler and Norman Ritchie in the USA; and other British collectors who loaned further items for photography: David Griffith and Ivan Taylor.

All the many international companies who loaned packs, supplied information and gave permission for their products to be reproduced here, especially: American Brands Inc, New York; Bacon's, Cambridge: Mrs Myers; British-American Tobacco, London: Brian Hearnshaw, John Palmer (particularly for the kind loan of their photograph album of BAT in China); Brown & Willamson Corporation, Kentucky; Carreras Rothmans Ltd, Aylesbury: Tom Dimmock, Jean Moore and Connie Sutton, Curator of the Niels Ventegodt Collection; Gallaher Ltd,

London; Gama Records Ltd, London (for permission to reproduce the Mirage album cover); Gitanes and Gauloises, London and Paris; Imperial Group, Bristol: Brian Freeman; Japanese Tobacco Corporation, Tokyo; Larus Bros Tobacco Co; Liggett Group, North Carolina (particularly for permission to reproduce the advertisement on page 104); Mardon, Son & Hall, Bristol: Bruce Young; Philip Morris Inc, New York; John Player & Sons, Nottingham: Alan Dobson; R J Reynolds Industries Inc, North Carolina (particularly for permission to reproduce their Camel pack on the front cover of the US and Canadian editions); Scotten-Dillon Co, Ohio; J L Tiedemann Tobakfabrik, Oslo: Sigmund Eikeland: Tillotson Carton Division, Liverpool: Howard Jamrack; US Tobacco Co, Connecticut; W D & H O Wills, Bristol: David Redway, Hubert Rudman, Bill Towers.

Those who worked so hard on the production of the book in both Britain and the USA: Ann Bond, Lynn Franklin, Diane Huntzicker and Georgiana Parry-Crooke for liaison and research; Reg Boorer for the design of the book; Bill Dare for the illustration on the title page and front jacket of the UK edition; Norman Hollands for the photography; and Charlotte Parry-Crooke for the editorial co-ordination of the project.

Finally Julianna Borsa, Paul Frewin, Donald Margulies and Robert Smith for all their useful suggestions. and Oriole Mullen for her company on pack expeditions, checking of the text and for her support throughout.

All the photographs in this book were taken by Norman Hollands except for those taken or kindly provided by the following: Chris Collins Studio, New York: 15 (top), 42, 50, 51, 52, 57 (top), 93, 94, 105, 108 (top), 116, 117, 125; Richard Denyer, Norwich: back flap; Michael Dyer Associates, London: 8 (top), 12, 15 (bottom), 17 (top), 28, 29, 92, 97, 99, 104, 110, 112; J L Tiedemans Tobakfabrik, Oslo: 69 (bottom left); W D & H O Wills Ltd, Bristol: 17 (bottom), 18 (left), 97.

PUBLISHERS' NOTE

Pack Dimensions: most of the cigarette packs reproduced in this book are shown as near life-size as possible. In some cases however, packs have been enlarged or reduced on account of the design of the book.

Correspondence: all correspondence concerned with this volume should be addressed to Ventura Publishing Ltd, London.

CONTENTS

INTRODUCTION

'Twenty times a day you take that pack out of your pocket. The average smoker smokes a pack a day. That pack has to stand for something. It takes on a personal association. That brand can't begin to stand for something that's a little embarrassing to you.' This book is not about the development of cigarette smoking, or about changes of fashion. It's about carrying with you a packet that has 'to stand for something', as a senior executive of Philip Morris put it in 1971.

The pack's function is to protect the contents; the images printed on it can have no effect on this function. Their role is at once frivolous and of great importance.

In a highly competitive market with such a range of brands, the design and visual identity of the pack are vital if a sale is to be made. The main part of this book looks at the various ideas and images that pack designers and advertisers have resorted to over the years, but the Introduction aims to give some idea of the technical expertise and artistic richness lavished on the cigarette. Because, for such an apparently simple product, the cigarette, the technology of packaging is one of great complexity, and an area of Design History rarely touched upon. Why this seeming indifference to such an important area of human affairs?

The cigarette pack does not feature in stories of heroic deeds. No sailor has saved himself from drowning by clinging to his pack of *Navy Cut*. No soldier has been saved from the firing squad by the thickness of his cigarette pack. Ironically, WD&HO Wills preserve a tin of *Three Castles* cigarettes pierced by a bullet hole which was removed with the cigarettes intact from the body of the unfortunate owner on the Western front during the First World War.

The very ordinariness of the cigarette pack – produced in its hundreds of millions every year, bought, used and then thrown away – has led to it being overlooked. It is no accident that no real-life spy scandal is complete without the unassuming but vital pack. In the Martelli spy case in Britain a soft pack of Philip Morris concealing a tiny book of codes became a vital piece of evidence for the prosecution when it turned out to be a pack that could only have been bought in Switzerland. A Russian defector from the KGB recently brought with him, he said, a soft pack of cigarettes that fired bullets. More worries for smokers.

For something so anonymous, the cigarette pack does carry with it many sources of information. Packs bought in London that carry the phrase '. . . the goods of the successors to . . .' might reveal the existence of a smuggling ring, as that phrase is only printed on packs destined for the export market. The slightest piece of the pack might help in dating an event. For instance, in Britain in the early 1970s a skeleton was found behind a bricked up fireplace. In a shred of jacket a piece of a *Crack Shot* pack was found, which John Palmer, head of British-American Tobacco's Trademark Division, and an internationally known expert on packaging, was able to date to the early 1920s, a period when the building was a pawnbroker's. The skeleton was probably that of a burglar who became trapped when he climbed down the chimney to rob the shop and found the fireplace walled up.

Yet, at the same time as packs, by their multiplicity, seem anonymous, just another piece of printed trivia in the pocket, they do, in certain circumstances, receive probably more attention than any other form of packaging. In the long hours on watch, soldiers and sailors sometimes had little else to look at but the pack in the pocket. This probably accounts for the flood of letters to cigarette companies pointing out inaccuracies in the designs of packs (see page 66: Player's *Navy Cut* and Wills' *Pirate*). Many people saw faces of women and lions, even a naked lady, in the scruffy hide of Old Joe, star of Reynolds' *Camel*.

Similarly, the mass distribution of packs has often led to their being used for propaganda purposes outside the tobacco industry, for example during the First World War (see page 38) and the Second World War (see page 103). In Communist countries packs have been used as an appeal for further national sacrifices and the glorification of the Mother Land.

Indeed even when there has been no such intention, hidden messages have been discerned by a watchful public. Wills found that the disturbance of the balance of the green and orange colours on their *Woodbine* packs immediately aroused suspicions among certain sections of the population in Northern Ireland. For years there has been a rumour there that the cross-shaped printer's registration mark on the glued edge of the pack meant that two pence of the purchase price went straight to the coffers of the Vatican.

Certain rumours can be dangerous. Even today, long after the coupon schemes of the 1930s that often promised that the front of packs could be redeemed for cash or gifts, modern British cigarette manufacturers still get sack loads of empty packs from charities and clubs, claiming their due, all based on a rumour.

Special Packs

'Special Packs' can be commemorative, promotional or propaganda devices. In the case of the American *Brand X* packs they can be a joke.

Commemorative packs are much more familiar to Old World smokers than to those in New and Third World countries. In America cigarette companies have consistently fought shy of celebrating an event, a triumph or a joy with special packs. Marketing techniques, which have always been more sophisticated, have led American tobacco firms to believe that nothing must impinge on the pack's identity. There is one refreshing exception to this rule, personalized packs, a service provided by several companies but principally by Your Name Cigarettes of Chicago (see overleaf). For every celebration in your life you could have a pack to remember it by – 'Happy 35th Anniversary Mom and Dad, 1916–1951?', – 'Cormier Family Reunion, Sept 27, 28, 1952'. Photographs of Your wedding, Your christening, could all appear as wrappings for 20 cigarettes. Companies equipped their salesmen with packs bearing their promotional message to the world, 'protecto Toilet Seat Covers – The Shield of Protection', '36% more distributors in Ohio sell Burkhard's Beer and Mug Ale than a year ago', 'Miracle, the adjustable all-in-one golf club'. Societies, hotels and organizations had their own packs made, as well as television stations and athletic clubs.

Packs have also played their part in

the political hard sell – 'Win with Nixon' shouted a flat box of 20 cigarettes shown here (An Exclusive Creation of the Nat Sherman Company). 'Let's Back Jack' shouted back an identically designed box of 20 cigarettes (An Exclusive Creation of the Nat Sherman Company). 'Stephenson for President' said one soft cup pack 'I like Ike' enthused another (right). For the winner there was the Presidential Pack specially made for the smoking incumbent. At a less exalted level, the Ace Calendar and Speciality Company produced a portrait pack, 'Elect Joe Runnels, Jr, A Proven Public Official'.

But in Europe the sight of the un-familiar on a standard brand has not daunted the manufacturer. Exhibitions and festivals have long sold souvenir packs. Standard brands like Holland's *Miss Blanche* have relished the opportunity afforded by such events as the Olympics, of linking the brand character (see pages 118–119) with something of public interest. On one pack the gregarious Miss Blanche is seen leaping through the Olympic hoops.

Most Old World commemoratives, however, celebrate the marriages and anniversaries of royalty – probably the few legitimate opportunities for cigarette companies to make overt royalist references. The *Jubilaum* pack on page 36 commemorates the Golden Wedding of King Christian IXth of Denmark and Queen Louisa in 1892. In 1936 the *State Express* brand (page 11) was permitted a beautifully designed box to commemorate the coronation of George VI. There is even a little known brand, *Anno Santo*, produced by the Vatican City to celebrate a Holy Year.

As well as the wealth of specialist packs, there is also the anti-pack. The *Brand X* pack (far right) aims to amuse, 'Costs a Little More – But Promises a little less. For the Man who is Satisfied with Nothing Less than Second Best'. But the *Cancer* pack (far right) had a different purpose. Bearing the standard Health Warning, the pack reads simply, 'Cancer Filter Cigarettes. A Daring Tobacco Combination.' Rather than being the ultimate marketing boob, along the lines of 'Cod Pieces', a proposed fish food novelty, the brand was designed to help the addicted but reluctant smoker to kick the habit. There is a similar more recent Dutch pack called *Mem-Mor (Memento mori –* remember that you must die) showing a skull with a rose in its teeth. Batt's *Wooden Kimona Nails* (page 42) could do the same thing in the 1920s without any fear of damaging sales.

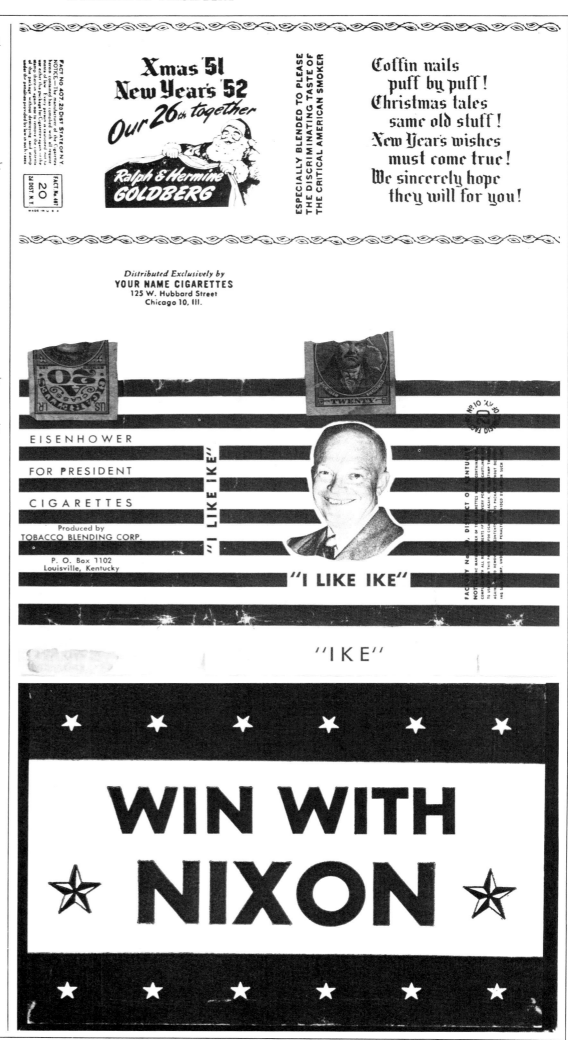

Pack Collections

The collecting habit has always been strong with tobacco products. Apart from pack inserts such as cigarette cards, mentioned below, the packs themselves, originally intended to be discarded once the product they preserved had been consumed, have been given a longer life for many reasons. The wealth of repeated imagery, the Player's Hero trademark, the celebrated silhouette of the *Camel*, the *Lucky Strike* bull's-eye, has been exploited by people covering trays, tables, bar-tops and even picture frames. People used to cut out every Hero they could find and arrange them

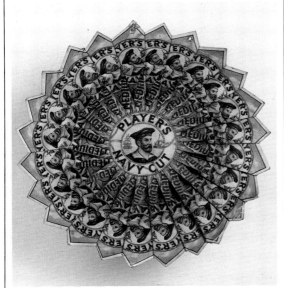

in spectacular geometric patterns. Kids still hoard packs for all manner of reasons, and more than a few pack enthusiasts have admitted that this was how they started their collections.

Cigarette packs themselves are now widely collected, though not to the same extent as cigarette cards. With the constant changes in our environment, the disappearance of familiar packaging, and the emergence of many new brands each year, there is a need to have easily available the paraphernalia of the past. Clothes, magazines, and, more recently, electric machines have been carefully conserved and studied, but not so cigarette packs, which probably had an equal impact on people's lives. They are, after all, remembrances of youthful thrills and can be just as representative of particular moments in people's lives.

The major collections of packs are held in private hands, or by institutions which need examples constantly on hand for the defence of their trademarks. The largest collection in the world, 52,160 different packs from 210 different countries, was assembled by the Danish lawyer, Niels Ventegodt.

His collection was acquired by Carreras-Rothman and, although it is still growing, it is fast being overtaken by at least two private collections in Britain. In America the collecting habit is more widespread and organized, with its own journal *Brandstand*, put together by a major collector, Richard Elliott. As yet no public museum has anything like a comprehensive collection of packs in their archives. This book aims therefore to show at least the full extent of this field of pack design for the collector, design historian, and general reader.

Pack Variations

The packaging of cigarettes is a reasonably straightforward business – the preservation of a product at a certain moisture level, and in a certain physical shape. But protection for the

cigarette has involved a fantastic number of shapes, sizes and media. In America there was an initial flirtation with the hull-and-slide, a two piece cardboard structure sometimes called the shell-and-slide, an outer casing acting as a wrapper to an inner card casing holding the cigarettes. More expensive cigarettes were sold in more substantial flat boxes with lids, often sophisticated in structure and design, and imitating the cigarette boxes found casually lying on coffee tables, provided either by the cigarette company or by the tobacconist who retailed his own brands.

With the emergence of brands such as *Camel*, *Lucky Strike* and *Chesterfield*, the soft cup came into fashion, a one piece paper and foil wrapping that was sometimes printed by the tobacco company itself, but more usually

delivered by a local printing company. Unlike the hull-and-slide, the soft cup has no moving parts, merely a wrapped top to be opened. In addition to the benefits of ease of assemblage, the soft cup does not shed bits of tobacco out of the bottom of the pack into the smoker's pocket. It is a traditional belief in the tobacco industry that the soft cup was taken to American hearts because it suited more informal clothing, such as the casual shirt with breast pocket, whereas the slab-like form of the hull-and-slide slotted neatly into the jacket pocket of the British gentleman. Apart from national preferences, there are pack variations to suit economic conditions – the simple 'paper 5', a folded length of paper holding 5 cigarettes, was the basic covering for cheaper cigarettes in the USA before 'Buck' Duke made card packs available to all (see page 26), and for many years in the United Kingdom with such popular brands as *Woodbine* and *Weights*. Despite the increasing sophistication of packaging, paper packs returned in the two World Wars.

With the paper packet and the flat box, the soft cup and the hull-and-slide, we have encompassed most of the types of packaging to be encountered in the cigarette industry. Before the advent of the multi-national hinged lid pack, (the so-called crush proof pack), there were variants on these four basic packings, for example the specially curved metal tins for 5 or 10 cigarettes that were shaped to fit the thigh pocket. But in commercial terms these boxes were very much in the minority. Air and moisture-proof tins were necessary for exporting to countries with uncertain climates and conditions. The major pack development after 1945 was the invention by Molins Ltd of the hinged lid carton, which incorporates great strength and protection with minimal material usage and waste.

If the paper 5 was a working class pack, and the soft cup and hull-and-slide appealed to the middle classes, was there an upper class pack? There were elaborate hull-and-slides, like Baker's *Selim II* (left), or cigar style cases like the American *Straight Cut* (far left). There were special Banquet Boxes of up to 500 cigarettes in plush silks meant to accompany the decanter round the dinner table. But all authorities agree that it was a trifle vulgar at the *best* occasions (before 1939) suddenly to produce a cigarette pack; of course the upper echelons of smokers preferred the cigarette case. For American women there was, in 1924, the *Terri Vanity*, a stylishly moulded case hanging from the wrist containing a powder compact on one side and a compartment for 5 cigarettes, keys and coins on the other. For the American gentleman of tone, there was the *Fillkwik Cigarette Case*, 'To the man who carries his cigarettes crumpled in a paper package, a Fillkwik cigarette case will be a prized and useful gift . . .' (1924). From his *Fillkwik* he may of course offer his *Marmay Monogram Cigarettes*, 'with personal crest, monogram, coat-of-arms etc'.

Mass production of cigarettes has from the beginning meant mass-production of packaging. Before 1900 some cigarettes were sold by weight. Heavily decorated wooden cabinets displayed a range of loose cigarettes in the tobacconist's shop in sliding drawers behind a glass front, which would be weighed up and tipped into small envelopes. But, apart from times of economic depression, and wartime conditions, cigarettes were not sold loose to any great extent after 1900.

To give some idea of the range of packaging required by the tobacco industry, it is interesting to take just one brand, Wills' *Gold Flake*. From 1883–5 the brand was available in paper 5s, then in cartons of 5, 7, 8, 9, and 10, to cater among other contingencies, for vending machines and the individual preferences of export markets. As well as in cartons of 17, 18, and 20, the brand was packaged in air-tight round tins of 50, cartons of 50, 100, and, in 1941, large cartons of 500 for sale in the canteens and messes of the armed forces. Wills' *Gold Flake* was also available in square tins of 100 and in ordinary tins, and enamelled tins of 150.

The Passage of the Pack from Printer to Consumer

All possible contingencies had to be met by the designers and printers of packaging, and the study of the developing technology is a fascinating subject. To simplify the complicated procedures involved in tracing the passage of the pack from the printer to the consumer, the journey has been divided into eight stages: a background to the printing of packs; the contribution of the artist; the shaping of the pack; delivery to the tobacco factory; the packing process; distribution, home and abroad; pack inserts; pack design and the fashions of today; the future of packs.

A Background to the Printing of Packs

Today, the graphic design of the cigarette pack can involve design agencies, carton manufacturers and the cigarette company. The major British carton manufacturers are Mardon, Son & Hall of Bristol, Robinson's of Bristol (now DRG Cartons), Tillotson's of Liverpool, Pembroke Packaging of London, and David S Smith of Neath. Firms such as these with their studios and artists can play a major role in pack design, using their expertise to translate the artists' conceptions into print. Mardon's, so closely associated with printing for all aspects of the tobacco industry are probably unique in the way they have established a specialist team to provide sketches, designs and artwork specifically for tobacco products.

Before the rapid expansion of the Advertising profession in the 1920s, little is known of those individuals who designed and formed the cigarette packs. The few scattered references that do exist before the 1920s, suggest that the printing companies themselves played a more prominent part than is generally recognized in the way packs looked.

In this historical survey Mardon's has been stressed for two reasons, the richness of their company records as published in the firm's magazine *The Caxtonian*, and the long and complicated relationship between the company and the Imperial Tobacco Company, (the huge group of British tobacco firms), and British-American Tobacco, (the largest tobacco company in the world), who between them sell extensively world wide. Of the packs reproduced in this book a great many were printed at Mardon's. And in America there is no equivalent, no one company that so dominates the industry – the national preference for soft cup packs in the past has not required the sort of printing skills needed for the complex pack such as the hull-and-slide, demanded by the British smoker. To be as objective as possible, it seems that before 1939 British packs generally aimed at more sophisticated colour printing, and a greater weight of complex decoration. Much of this skill and craftsmanship, this visual flair originated with Mardon's.

When the age of the machine-made cigarette dawned in the 1880s, Mardon's was a substantial printing firm, an old established company specializing in stationery, headed notepaper, invoices and the like. The rival Bristol firm of Robinson's was also founded on stationery. Elisha Smith Robinson and his brother began their commercial careers buying plain paper, printing it with decorations and selling it from a barrow to shopkeepers. This trade led naturally to the Robinsons being commissioned by satisfied customers to print specially designed bags for wrapping. Mardon's too seem to have entered the packaging business in a similar way, with a special little sideline in printed tea papers that could be folded into cartons.

As early as 1849, Mardon's had realised the importance of lithography – for greater accuracy and longer runs in printing than the older processes such as engraving. And, as Heber Mardon, the major force behind the firm, wrote in his company history, 'from this date we never looked back.' The acquisition of a new steam driven lithographic machine direct from the makers in Paris in 1864, and the lithographic experience of Heber Mardon himself, prepared the firm for the sudden expansion of business brought about by contact with the cigarette industry.

Not surprizingly in a city so closely connected with the tobacco trade, Mardon's had found themselves as early as the 1850s printing for Franklyn & Co of Bristol, large numbers of 1 ounce and 2 ounce packets for tobacco. The device of the negro's head, a traditional emblem of the trade (see page 61), was printed in orange-red on paper; these were known as 'red heads.' However in 1883–4 Mardon's were approached by Mr H H Wills, manager of the nearby 'Virginia Cavendish Works', who needed some cardboard boxes for the newly established cigarette trade.

The contacts increased and, with the expansion of the business, Mardon's had to move its box making department to larger premises. 'We there made our *Woodbine* packets on small blocks, and on this work some of the young girls grew quite expert, and later on when paper mouthpieces came in vogue we made those by hand with a small tapered spindle turned by the fingers . . .'

Soon Mardon's were spreading their activities to machine production of paper mouthpieces for cigarettes, to showcards and novelties, (see page 98), and, from 1889, to the production of 'stiffeners', or cigarette cards. Contacts were established with American printing firms and cigarette manufacturers. A London office opened in 1895, a sure sign of success. It was only two years later that Tillotson's, another important cigarette packaging firm, began production of their carton range in a four-storey wharehouse in Salop Street, Bolton, using cigarette carton machines

imported from America.

For many people the period before the First World War was a golden age in the history of posters, packaging and advertising. Yet so little is known of the techniques and attitudes of the artists and printers responsible. We are lucky to have an eye witness account recorded in 1897 by a writer for *Tobacco* magazine, who was escorted around Mardon's premises. This will be quoted extensively in the sections which follow. The writer first gives us an astonishing list of the range of Mardon's productions. 'Here are Wills, Ogden's, Clarke, Anstie, Churchman, Hignett, Gloag, Baker, Godfrey Phillips, TSS, Hudden, Adkin, the American Tobacco Company, Bell, Kinnear, Edwards Ringer & Bigg, Hill, Archer, Morris, Pritchard & Burton, Fraenkel, Mitchell, Gallaher, Hodge, H J Nathan, Fryer & Sons, Fryer & Coultman, Smith, Strauss of Bloemfontein, Player, Mason, Robinson & Sons, Robinson & Barnsdale, Muratti, Kriegsfeld, Macdonald, Harvey & Davy, J Biggs, Taddy, Cope, Lambert & Butler, Banks & James, Brankston, Lloyd, Milligan, Faulkner, and everybody else in the trade, all lying contentedly together. The puzzle would be to find a firm of any standing that is not represented in this box of specimens.' If nothing else, this roll of honour gives some idea of the vigour of the British tobacco firms before the invasion of the American Tobacco Trust, (see pages 28–9), and the creation of the Imperial Tobacco Company in 1901 (see also pages 28–9).

'Right and left of the front entrance are respectively the Counting House and Sale Room . . . A glance into an adjacent part of the factory brings to light the men who prepare the litho stones for receiving fresh transfers and those who grind the immense quantities of coloured inks used in the place. For, excepting ordinary black, Messrs Mardon, Son & Hall prefer to make their own inks. Close at hand, in a fine, light room, are the artists, some two dozen of them, engaged in various operations . . .'

The writer then went through the litho machine room, with 'machines turning out piles upon piles of large printed sheets, which have to be cut up into slips for making into cigarette packages . . .' Nearby was the bronzing department through which the printed sheets passed for those extra touches of lustrous colour such as can be seen on pages 30–1. Packs such as Ogden's *Lucky Star* which had a large bronze coin on the front, were printed in this department. 'The bronze is applied by machine, a much more rapid method than the old fashioned way of dusting it on by hand. The quantity of bronze used by Messrs Mardon, Son & Hall is simply astonishing. They order it by the ton, whereas twenty years ago, (said Mr Harris), it was difficult to get him to order more than 14 or 28 lbs at a time.'

The penny packet making machine held a special fascination for him – 'little girls feed the papers in at one side of the machine at a rate of 30,000 a day for each machine, and underneath, the complete packages drop out; the packets made by this machine have the seam at the sides, which, of course, means so much additional strength.'

Next came the carton department 'where numerous ingenious machines are employed in turning out the millions of slide boxes which nowadays are a matter of such necessity to all manufacturers of cigarettes.' In another section he observed the mouthpiece machines. Nineteenth century cigarettes, both hand and machine made, did tend to be loosely packed and the smoker could, after a vigorous puff, find himself with a mouthful of tobacco. To counteract this nauseating experience, and to increase the hygienic aspects of smoking, mouthpieces were stacked in the cigarette pack, one for each cigarette on some brands, restricted on others. They could be either paper or cork. Fifty mouthpiece machines were running at the time of his visit. 'Each machine turns out many thousands of mouthpieces a day. The tips are subsequently dipped into a cauldron of melted paraffin wax, and then put into racks to dry. The way in which the mouthpieces are packed for delivery deserves notice. They are thrown into a large box which, by an ingenious internal contrivance, causes the pointed ends to insert themselves into the wider apertures, so that eventually long lengths of them can be taken out of the box, broken into twenties, and packed in boxes of 5000.' The more expensive brands contained a tip for each cigarette, but more often three were included in a 2d packet of 10, and 2 in each 1d packet of 5.

In addition to printing packets ready for dispatch to the cigarette companies, (at this time they were sent already made up with slide in hull), Mardon's offered an odd little sideline, the dummy packet (see *Bandmaster* overleaf). 'Here are a bevy of damsels busily engaged in filling with sawdust the packages of a variety of firms – packages which later on will, perhaps, be provocative of much bad language from members of the light fingered fraternity who may happen to extract them from a shop counter when the tobacconist is not looking.'

In the year in which this article appeared Mardon's had become a limited liability company with a capital of £200,000. By 1901 the firm was so crucial to the future of the British industry that, in the face of the American Tobacco Company's invasion of Britain, it was incorporated into the newly formed Imperial Tobacco Company (on January 1, 1902). With their stocks of paper and board, Mardon's were a prime target for 'Buck' Duke. It is indicative of the bitter warfare waged between Duke and Imperial that, after Mardon's had signed a three year contract with the Swedish mill of Lundgren, the American Trust first tried to buy up the mill's production for three years and, failing in that, then unsuccessfully tried to buy up the complete company.

Before 1900 most lithographic printing was from heavy, porous stones, specially imported from Germany. In 1899 Mardon's was the first firm in Europe to change to a machine that used a sheet of aluminium wrapped around the cylinder of the printing machine. The benefits were enormous; rotary printing was faster and more convenient than flat bed printing on heavy, cumbersome litho stones.

By the time Lionel Underhill, (whose account of his work at Mardon's is printed in *The Caxtonian*), joined the firm in 1905, rotary printing was well established. He remembered when, as an apprentice, he was asked to make transfers of the *Woodbine* designs from the original stones for translation to the big rotary machines. 'Unknown to any one, I used to buy my own salts from the chemist, making my own etch, and soon gained a reputation from machine minders for good plates that did not scum . . .' Apart from the standard British brands of the day such as *Woodbine* and *Gold Flake*, Mr Underhill also handled British-American Tobacco brands including *Flag*, *Polo* and *Akbar Shah*. Some of the most complicated work he handled involved cigarette cards, 'usually printed in twelve colours with descriptive texts on the back. You had to be most careful that the type matter corresponded with the fronts.'

Despite the new machines, the printing processes were painstakingly slow when compared with production speeds today. The firm not only made its own inks, and stored and matured its supplies of card for up to a year, but was even forced at times to wait until temperature and atmospheric pressure within the factory were exactly right before the ink could be applied. Some cigarette packs were printed in anything up to six to eight colours, and 24 hours or even longer had to be allowed for each colour stage to dry.

Although there were several new technical developments to be absorbed into production of packaging, (including the introduction of tissue backed foil by the firm in 1926, and, in the same year, of transparent wrapping film, such as 'cellophane'), basically the same printing and carton making machines were used up to the 1950s, when new machines were installed to cater for the expansion of the packaging industry after the war. A modern printing firm specializing in cartons must operate a full range of printing and finishing machinery if it is to provide the versatility needed to meet the varied demands of the industry. Litho and Letterpress are still extensively used, but more recently the increased use of foil board and greater emphasis on gold print has brought an upsurge in the demand for Gravure. Whilst much of this requirement is met from sheet fed machines, a number of printers operate Rotagravure machines. Here a reel of board is fed in at one end, and finished blanks, printed in up to 6 colours and varnished, punched, embossed and stripped are delivered out of the other.

Having given some brief account of the demands made upon printing companies by the consumer society, we come now to the question of the designs themselves.

The Contribution of the Artist

The writer for the *Tobacco* magazine had noticed some two dozen artists working at Mardon's. 'The number seemed prodigious even for this huge concern, but when I mention that for an ordinary showcard in colours there are a dozen or more different workings required, each necessitating the transference of a separate portion of the design, it will be seen that a marvellous quantity of delicate work, some of it almost microscopic in its smallness, has to be got through.' The same artists who worked on the showcards would also be required to produce cigarette cards and the cigarette packs themselves. In the early days, around 1900, before the adoption of photolithography, which was mainly a mechanical process, the artist's task included not only pattern making, figure drawing and lettering, but great precision drawing on the separate litho stones. 'Casting my mind back,' Lionel Underhill says, 'I marvel at the skill of the chromo artists in drawing such minute meticulously accurate figures and designs on lithographic stones . . .'

Where did all these artists come from? Where did they acquire that astonishing vocabulary of forms that so marked cigarette packs throughout the world before rationalization and marketing caused the removal of decoration and figurative imagery?

In Britain, after a Governmental Committee on Arts and Manufactures had shown in 1836 that designers were not being trained for industry, Schools of Design were set up all over the country. Although not as broadly based as some Continental Schools, they did at least give many young men contact with a wider range of visual material than they would have met with in industry alone. Many artists of distinc-

tion worked as designers for industry before 1900, Alfred Stevens for the Iron Founders Hoole & Company of Sheffield, Thomas Jeckyll for Barnard, Bishop & Barnard of Norwich, manufacturers of decorative iron work.

Another factor in the increasing awareness in Britain of the need to incorporate design departments within the industrial process, was the availability of pattern books to a greater extent than ever before, and with it a developing chromo lithographic industry. Talk to printers or artists responsible for creating packaging designs and quite a number will admit to having at their elbow the most comprehensive of these pattern books, Owen Jones' *Grammar of Ornament* (1856).

Owen Jones (1809–1874) had travelled widely through Europe and the Middle East after his apprenticeship to the architect Lewis Vulliamy. He had little success as an architect but because of his immense experience in studying applied decoration he was encouraged to publish his researches. His *Plans, Elevations, Sections and Details of the Alhambra*, printed by chromo-lithography in 1842, popularized a taste for the Hispano-Moresque style. As a lecturer he talked to learned societies and Working Men's Colleges. As an interior decorator he was responsible for the colour scheme in the interior of the Crystal Palace in 1851, and the decorative features of the St James Music Hall. As a designer he illustrated and embellished several books, and produced many different wall-papers, textiles, carpets, tissues and, more important for the purpose of this book, playing card backs and packages for biscuit manufacturers.

But it was his monumental work, *Grammar of Ornament*, that had most impact on designers. The book, originally published in large folio parts, showed for the first time ornaments from all over the world. The 3000 illustrations reproduced examples of designs from China and the Far East, from the Middle East and India, as well as the usual range of Western patterns. The collection could have created confusion, such was the wealth of material, had it not been for the 37 Propositions, or aesthetic guidelines, printed at the beginning of the book. If the rich, ornate patterning of the packs in this book has a unity and balance, Owen Jones' great manual of ornament may not only have provided designs, but also an aesthetic control.

Grammar of Ornament was in its

original format too large for practical use. In 1865 the book was published as a small folio, with several plates combined. It is indicative of how successive generations found use for the small folio that it was reprinted in 1910 and again in 1972. Jones' influence was felt not only in Europe; a number of American designers used his plates, particularly in the creation of the flat box of Turkish cigarettes with exotic, even bizarre imagery (see page 117). The *Murad* pack, (below; see also page 116), is a startling example of the

influence of Jones' book, as well as of the way in which packs are designed. The front of the pack has a curious mixture of Egyptian bits and pieces, real and imagined. When the artist came to design the back, he seems to have chosen a more bare desert scene to contrast with the clutter of the front. To add strength to the edges he decided to use two columns to flank the scene. Probably not feeling too confident about Egyptian architecture – look at the structure on the front, a chess piece or perhaps a coal bunker – he must have

picked up his *Grammar of Ornament* and turned to the Egyptian plates. Flicking back from the five crammed pages of abstract patterning, he must have stumbled on Plate VI (left) showing pairs of columns from Egyptian temples. In the Introduction to the Egyptian section he might have read that the columns could be as small as a few feet high, or as big as 40 or 50 feet. On the bottom of the page to left and right can be found two designs with fractionally more shaft to the column and more definite shape to the capital. This pair of columns has been transferred exactly to the *Murad* pack. The column shafts were extended downwards; in the process establishing a correct perspective to the bases turned out to be quite a difficult task. But the pack at least had its vertical stresses across which to hang the brand name.

For British commercial artists there

15

were even more examples of ornament available, such as Pugin's *Glossary of Ecclesiastical Ornament* (1844) and Wyatt's *The Art of Illuminating* (1860), both produced with precise register and brilliant clarity of colour. Such was the reputation of British chromo-lithographic artists and printers that the pioneer French poster artist Jules Cheret chose to come to London to learn his trade.

Apart from the more usual influences on pack art, the exuberance of letter forms shown in a pack like Lloyd's *Porpoise* (page 32), the chunky, cheeky flourish of the numbers '20 for 3d', the almost human qualities of the lettering of the brand name, suggest that packs may also show the influence of what was probably the most vital area of popular design before the First World War, the Comic. In this period both commodities can largely be called amenities enjoyed by the working classes. A caricature of the British gentleman of the middle classes would surely show him at this time with a pipe rather than a cigarette and with *Punch* rather than *Comic Cuts*. The rise of the Comic, its early days with the launch of *Funny Folks* (1874), and proliferation during the 1890s, corresponds with the rise of the cigarette. That they were aiming at generally the same clientele may be belied by some of the aristocratic brand names of the cigarettes but not by the exuberance of the lettering, love of curling, entwined decoration that surrounds it, and the occasional appearance of a comic book character, as in *Footprints* (see page 31) and *Latchkey* (page 32). The *Tit Bits* pack (page 25) seems to make this exact point; a jaunty fish boy has sat down on the steps to read his comic, leaving his tray unattended. A prowling cat is about to benefit. It's a scene straight out of the Comics. And perhaps the same tendency can be seen in American packs of the period. The Consolidated's *The New Wrinkle* (page 27) shows a rakish clown leering out at the world, his hands in his pockets, with a comic truculence often seen in the last frame of some strip cartoon. The resemblance is increased by the anarchic behaviour of the lettering – the coiled springs of the 'N' and 'E' shooting up and down to rock the symmetry of the pack. The maker's name joins in with a repetition of curled 'C's, and even the frame with whippy curlicues that terminate in an aimless doodle. Exactly the same effects are seen in the early comics, where no single letter leaves the others alone.

The comic tradition survived into the 1920s and beyond with Batt's *Wooden Kimona Nails* (page 42) and *Bonnell Blend* (page 44). Probably the most deliberate evocation of the comic world is that extraordinary pack, or rather flat box label, *The Blue Horse Pills*, with its strong but sensitive outline filled with washes of colour (page 44).

The other influences on the artists who worked on pack designs were perhaps more traditional. Apprentices were taken on by the firm for training, and artists were lured from other industries. In his history of Mardon, Son & Hall, published in 1918, Heber Mardon noted that with the increase of cigarette work, greater demands were put on all departments of the firm. 'With the superior colour work we were now successfully doing, our artistic staff became larger, and in 1883 Mr F S Ringham came to us from Harrison's of Bradford. We had others of our own training such as Bailey and Bowden, but they had not the stable mind of Mr Ringham, and their tastes were far too Bohemian to make them reliable so they drifted away. We had a Frenchman also who was very clever as an artist, but whose temper was such that he worked in a small room partitioned off. An incident occurred which indirectly led to his leaving rather abruptly. Being in his own room, he had evidently ignored the time for leaving, and paid no attention to the bell, so that he got locked in, and the factory being some distance back from the street, he could not make himself heard. I believe he had to remain there all night until the factory was reopened in the morning.'

Bohemians and peppery Frenchmen apart, there was another source of design expertise that must be noted, the decorative artist already within the printing trade. Such was Harry Close who, before joining Mardon's, had worked as an artist creating illuminated addresses, specializing in intricate scroll work and grandiose lettering. His subsequent career illustrates the changing role of the artist. He began as a litho designer; this was exacting work since everything had to be drawn in reverse ready for direct printing from the stone. When, after the First World War, photography began to make a greater contribution to the litho process, he turned to photo-litho retouching.

In 1948, the firm's journal noted that 'recent years have seen a remarkable development in photo-lithography. In this process, the sketch is photographed in the camera room on sensitized glass

plates which are then carefully retouched by expert artists before being printed onto metal in the printing down room . . . In the mass production of labels, cartons, etc where accurate register (the exact colour fitting of one colour area to another) is of paramount importance, the Photo-Litho Section utilizes precision machines of the most modern type. Multiple negatives are made in which each individual label or carton is mechanically positioned, and it is from such negatives that machine plates of extreme accuracy of register are produced for the litho printing machines.'

The role of the artist has changed over the years, the meticulous drawing required for lithography is a thing of the past, but the artists' department is still a major factor in cigarette pack production. It is the width of a stripe as determined by market research rather than the precise contortions of the ribbon which is of paramount importance today.

The Shaping of the Pack

In recent years, with the introduction of the new hinged lid pack, production has been somewhat simplified. The pack is printed, scored and left flat, ready for delivery to the cigarette factory where it is wrapped around the cigarettes at the end of the manufacturing process. The American soft cup is equally uncomplicated to produce. Cigarette firms usually take delivery of the standard wrappings, the inner roll of foil and paper laminate, a paper wrapper with designs on side and bottom, and the final wrapping of film. These materials are easily injected into the manufacturing process.

To the usual process of wrapping *Lucky Strike*, the American Tobacco Company boast the addition of a little automatic detector. 'As the paper and foil are rolled to make a pack of 20 cigarettes, 20 metal fingers reach out and touch the ends of each. If there is a defect in any single cigarette, a light flashes and a little arm, a second later, throws the whole pack into the discard.'

Compared with the paper pack the hull-and-slide (preferred until recently in Britain, France and Ireland) required greater technology. Two separate and quite independent units have to be made and supplied ready for assemblage. A description of the carton and folding box department at Mardon's in 1949 shows how complicated this process has been. Printed and cut sheets were fed into the 'Baron machine' that 'creases, glues, folds, refolds and

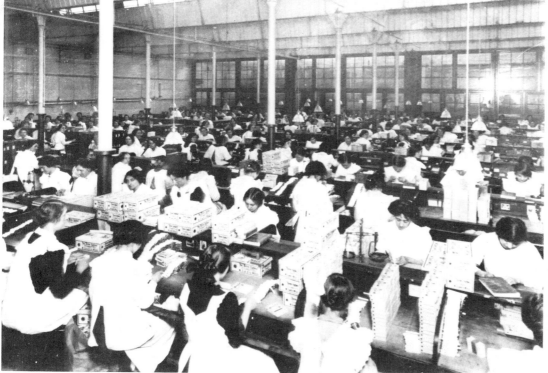

and horse could be hired with no stabling accommodation or veterinary services to be provided, for these were the responsibilities of the contractor.' In 1912, however, the decision was taken to buy a 3 ton Halley Van. 'It was fitted, of course, with solid tyres and there was chain transmission. Two men, Walter Clements and William Hann, were trained as driver and vanguard.'

Once in the factory the packs are then stored ready for loading into the packing machines. Innovations such as the tissue-backed foil and transparent wrapping film have necessitated changes in the packing process. Packs were specially altered to cater for every extra internal thickness, no matter how slight. Even when a pack had to contain a cigarette card the machinery had to be adapted to make it a fraction bigger.

The filling process at the cigarette factories was, until the First World War, generally done by hand (top left: at one of BAT's 'factories' in China; bottom left: in a more organized manner at Wills in Bristol), but the increasing use of advanced machinery virtually eliminated manual operation. From 1924 onwards it was possible to link cigarette manufacture and packing in the same process.

Cigarette firms took natural pride in their packs, and when a new brand was launched the pack was emphasized as much as the cigarette itself. For instance in June 1955, when the country was still suffering austerity, the British firm of Marcovitch took a three page supplement in *Picture Post* to announce the launch of their *Red and White* cigarette. Showing photographs of the packing process, the company assured the world that '*Red and White have* got something to offer beside the novelty of a good packet.'

Distribution, Home and Abroad

On their packs and on their advertisements, some tobacco companies like to convey the image of the monumental scale of their operations. In a futurist fancy published in 1921 in the *Illustrated News*, Major Drapkin & Co publicized their *Greys* cigarettes with 'Greys' Anticipations No 5' showing their factory in the year AD 2500. The monolithic metropolis sucks in tobacco supplies from the air while long motorized torpedos speed away huge containers of cigarettes.

While on not quite as grandiose a scale as Drapkin's dream, the distribution system at the *Lucky Strike* factory was described in awed terms by Roy C Flanagan (1938). 'Deft women pack

cuts them into single hulls, finally counting them . . .' Slides were produced from reels 'which are fed into machines fitted with a roller carrying steel engravings for printing, and a second roller to cut, crease and emboss, the waste material being removed at the same time.' They were then tied up into bundles and dispatched to the cigarette firms which had ordered them.

Delivery to the Tobacco Factory; the Packing Process

Deliveries from printing firms to the factories are usually run on a daily basis, such is the constant demand. Before 1912, Mardon's delivered to other Bristol-based members of the Imperial group in a fleet of horse-drawn vehicles hired from a local carrier, J C Wall & Co. 'For a charge of from £3 to £3.10s.0d weekly, man, boy them in their cartons (there were ten packs to the carton) and the cartons in turn are stowed away in boxes containing fifty cartons, or ten thousand cigarettes. Out into the world they move like a mighty army – carload after carload . . . they are then shipped to the four corners of America and to the ends of the earth.'

The large cardboard boxes would then go to the wholesalers and then to the retailer. At the tobacconist's the packs would be stored or displayed.

Many features outside (below) or in the shop would remind the customer of a particular brand; he or she might walk in through a door decorated with pelmets or transparencies, brush past showcards, flags, novelties and streamers. The packs were stacked behind the counter but could also be featured on a counter card (filled with sawdust of course). Tired by all this, the smoker might find himself sitting in a special Wills' *Woodbine* chair and, searching for visual peace, look up to

see an advertising ceiling where packs and handbills were stuck to the separate panels. Tobacconists vied with each other in the construction of pack displays showing, say, all of Player's tobacco products in complicated pyramids of packs, tins, boxes

and wrappers (above).

The other major destination of those marching armies of cardboard boxes was the Export market. The biggest exporter of cigarettes is, of course, the British-American Tobacco Company, formed in 1902 as part of the settlement between the warring British and American tobacco industries (see page 35). By the outbreak of the First World War BAT had such an extensive network of distribution that they acted for Wills when that firm was given huge orders for cigarettes by the British government for the troops. In peacetime, BAT exported hundreds of brands to virtually every country in the world. One of the largest markets was pre-Revolutionary China (see pages 20–21). Cases of cigarettes were landed at the ports and transferred to railway wagons specially painted with the company's name. At the end of the railway system the cargo was loaded onto camel trains, said to be the longest in the world, destined for the country's northernmost provinces. Although BAT found it more economic to build factories and printing works in countries of consumption, the extent of their export trade from Britain and the USA was always immense. You can get some idea of the scale of the company's operations by looking at the brands available from an American catalogue of about 1920. To the South American

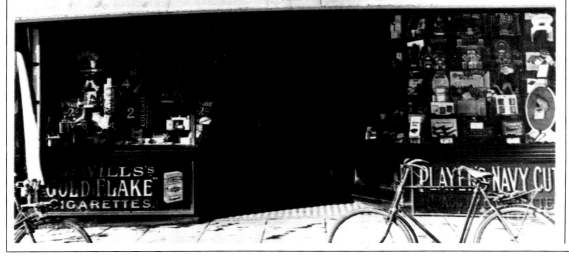

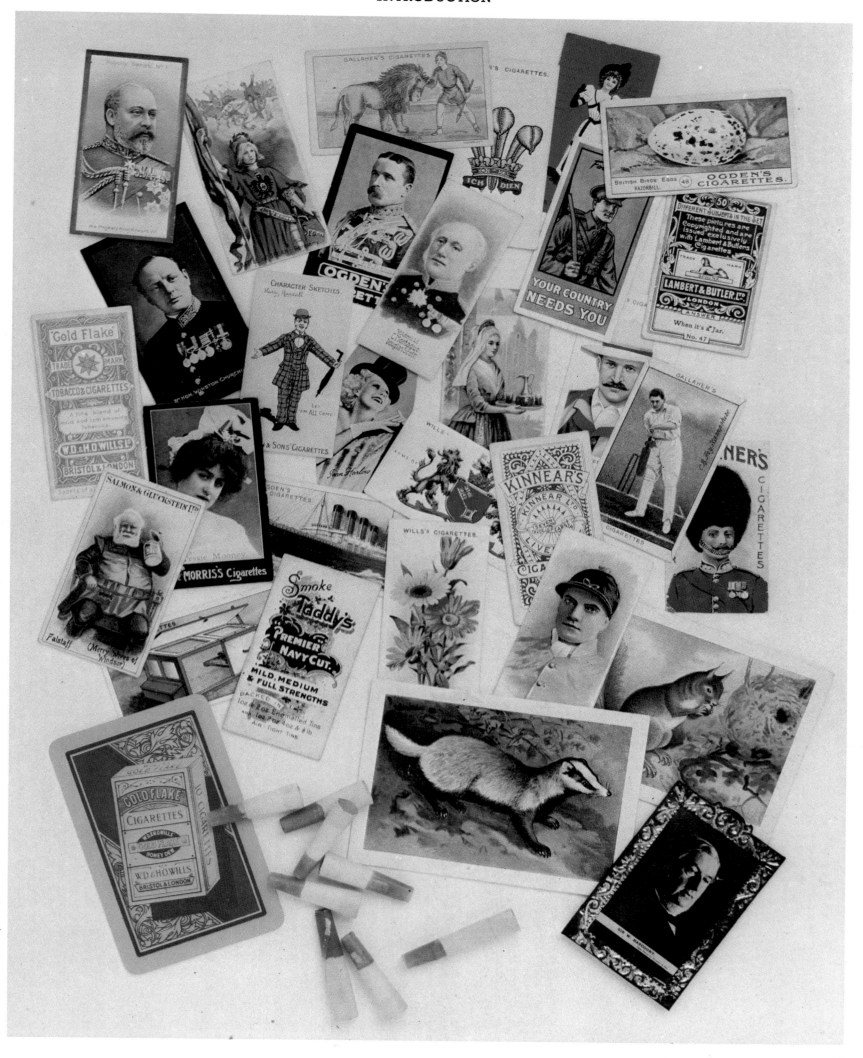

market, BAT offered *Cross Cut*, *Cycle*, *Eagle*, *Emu*, *Fatima*, *Hassan*, *High Flyer*, *Home Run*, *King Bee*, *Lucky Strike*, *Murad*, *New York*, *Piedmont*, *Pin Head*, *Richmond*, *Sweet Caporal*, *Turkish Trophies* and *Escobal's Virginia Extra*. This was their full range of Virginia, Burley, Turkish blend and straight Turkish cigarettes. A popular brand such as *Murad* (see pages 116–17) 'filled from end to end with the best quality Turkish tobacco' was packed in cartons of 100 and tins of 500, inside cases measuring 10 ft 7 in square or 22 ft 5 in square. 'Upon request we gladly attend to shipping arrangements, insurance etc, thereby relieving our customers of the detailed work.'

It seems a tragedy that after this long journey, that product of precision engineering should lie in gutters, bins, country lanes, car boots and coal buckets, waiting for destruction or decay. Only in such a destructive civilization as ours could there be such a waste of resources and such a blasé disregard of printed imagery. In previous centuries, when technology of printing was not so advanced, designed and printed images were hoarded and treasured.

Pack Inserts

Before a last word on the modern pack, it seems unfair to talk about packaging without a brief reference to that very necessary element contained within, the free gift. The care and craftsmanship that were lavished on the packs, were, as we have seen, applied equally to those small colourful inducements intended to lure the smoker into the collecting habit, or put pressure on him from younger members of the family.

There were several kinds of induce-ment. With *Gainsborough* cigarettes you got a small photographic portrait of a personality of the day with an ornate frame in cheap metal. There were hundreds of coupon schemes (see page 96) in most countries, offering clothes, kitchen equipment and even clocks. Certain American brands offered miniature flags, little blankets and, with the American Tobacco Company's *Sovereign* cigarettes, tiny rugs in gaudy colours. Wills offered pack-sized playing cards which when the series was complete could be ex-changed for a full sized version.

But the most widespread pack insert was the cigarette card, intended originally as a cardboard stiffener for paper packs (previous page). American companies offered Famous Generals, Ships, Actresses and Flags. British firms

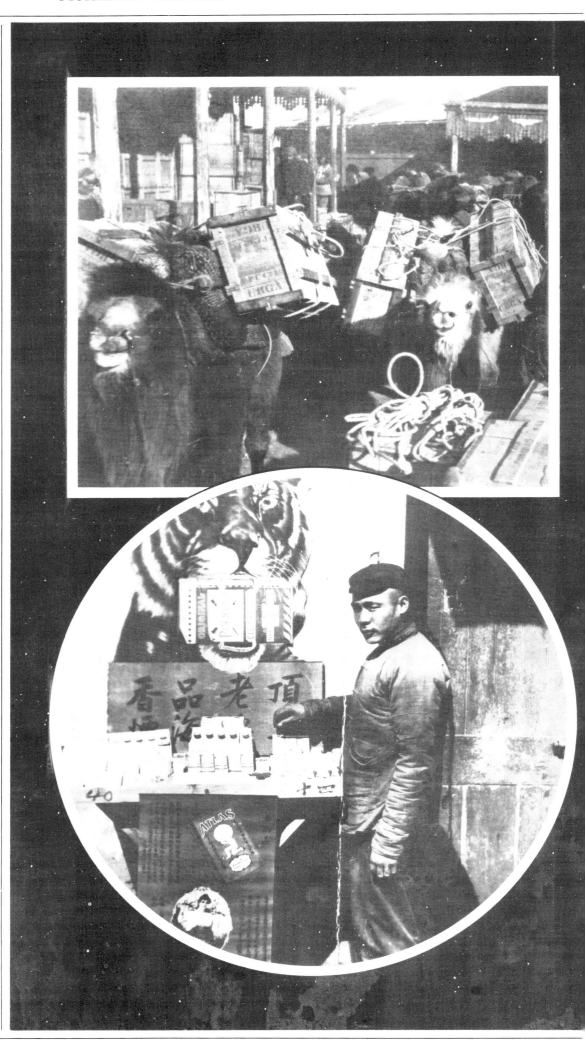

offered the same range of subjects. It became a national craze, and, although it narrowed the distance between smoking and the young, did put across well-researched and intelligent information. In 1939 production of cards was discontinued because of the war. It did not really revive afterwards. The cigarette industry itself was in a state of technological change, with the shift to the king size brand and the filter. There was little room for the insert.

Pack Design and the Fashions of Today

The major share of world cigarette packing goes to the soft pack, dominating the American market and occupying 54% of the European. The soft packs for the cheaper cigarettes can be as simple as a single sheet of paper with a sealing tag. The primitive single sheet soft pack is fast disappearing because of its often tawdry appearance. Recently the Italian tobacco monopoly has decided to make home brands as appealing as possible to counteract the huge smuggling industry that supplies preferred foreign cigarettes and packs. Generally, the cheaper pack associated more with Belgium and Italy is giving way to the more elaborate American-style packs, soft pack and hinged lid, with greater use of transparent film wrapping than ever before.

For more expensive modern cigarettes, an inner foil layer and an outer transparent film are added to the single paper sheet. Although there are definite advantages in the adoption of soft packs, cheaper to produce, easier to wrap, the pack also answers perhaps deeper psychological needs. Its use demands a sophisticated set of gestures, the great arc of the hand taking off the tear strip, and the subtle tapping on the pack to induce one cigarette to rise above the others. Unlike the flicking of a cigarette from a hinged lid pack, or a ritual unwrapping of the hull-and-slide, handling of the soft pack still has associations of Gangster Cool, particularly in Europe. Nobody would dream of narrowing their eyes in a look of wariness as they took a cigarette from a hull-and-slide with their lips.

The hull-and-slide pack accounts for about 10% of the European market, mainly bought by British, French and Irish smokers. It is very much a matter of regional preference, of traditional habits. For instance, as mentioned later on, Player's tried to bring in a hinged lid pack for their *Navy Cut* cigarettes, but the British public much preferred the hull-and-slide and the 'flip-top' had to be withdrawn. However other brands such as Wills' *Three Castles* long associated with the hull-and-slide, have made a successful transition.

Perhaps at this point, in discussing types of packaging, it might be interesting to look at how the transition from one pack type to another has affected design. Take as an example *Three Castles*, Wills' higher priced brand, which in 1956 changed from its familiar hull-and-slide to hinged lid. The first hinged lid and the revized version as seen today are shown on page 60.

The 1956 pack had to keep the original familiar Bristol harbour scene, but the new lid required changes – the whole scene had to be compressed on to the body of the pack, leaving the brand name on the lid. The revized version shows the brand name dropping on to the body of the pack where it was not obscured every time a cigarette was offered.

The concept of hinged lid cigarette packing was developed before 1939 but it was not really until after 1950 that the new pack came to be accepted, then, among certain groups of smokers, actively preferred. It has the benefits of the soft pack, in price, ease of assemblage and containment of loose tobacco, but has more associations of stylishness, with its solidity, and glossy, often metallic surfaces. The gesture of the arrogant flick of the thumb as the lid is thrown back is a familiar spectacle.

The hinged lid pack has about 31% of the market. The remaining types of packaging, 5% of the total, are mainly flat 20 metal boxes, round tins of 50 and the domed flat box, 'the Laube pack', more used for chocolates than cigarettes today. These last three types are really unsuitable for the mass-production required of the modern cigarette industry.

All three major types of cigarette packaging tend to be wrapped in transparent film today. This has often been criticized as being a luxury gloss to the pack, another unnecessary part of the wasteful ritual. It should not really be needed in temperate climates, but in specific circumstances, such as outdoor vending machines susceptible to extremes of heat and atmosphere, it may be necessary. New developments in the production of this film have created a wrapping that does not shrink and mangle the product. Much of the film used today in Europe is anti-static, a refinement that prevents the dust from penetrating the cigarette packing process.

We have already noticed national differences in pack preference – there is another area of packaging today that reveals startlingly different attitudes to smoking. Despite all attempts, cigarette buyers in the European Community have resisted all efforts to induce them to buy cartons of 200 cigarettes, a prominent feature of American life. This new object aversion has one psychological explanation. The European smoker's trip to buy his cigarettes each day is a valued ritual not to be surrendered to the weekly visit to the supermarket. The purchase of the pack is still very much a male preserve.

The Future of Packs

The packaging industry is, despite its advanced technology, basically a conservative one. In the past fifty years only the transparent wrapping film and the hinged lid pack have disturbed the world of the soft pack and hull-and-slide.

Two possible innovations are already being tried in America, the thermo-formed plastic pack that reduces the cost of trimming, printing and folding, and the one-piece 4-layered laminate of transparent film, polyethylene, printed aluminium, with another layer of polyethylene. These packs have apparently not been marketed elsewhere.

Rather than to technical innovation we must look to further extension of existing trends, to perhaps even more sophisticated packs (in structure and art) in countries such as France and Italy that have long resisted lavish cigarette packaging. Paradoxically the major European private enterprise companies may, in a harsher economic climate, with expected changes in tax structures, be forced to curtail some of the luxurious packaging insisted on by smokers, and particularly those in Britain. In 1975 about 27,800 million retail packs were produced for cigarette products within the Common Market. In Britain, carton production alone is worth £44–5 million per annum.

With the size of the packaging industry and its capital investment, it seems inconceivable that radical changes can come about. The adoption of more utilitarian packaging by companies has not met with much favour from the public who require still that container that can flatter or titillate.

Cigarettes probably more than any other consumer product bought on a daily basis need this extra visual and tactile stimulus. The modern cigarette carton is not just a container, 'It has to have a personality.'

Further Reading

Alford, B W E
W D & H O Wills and the Development of the UK Tobacco Industry
Methuen, London, 1973

Beatty, J
Our 100th Anniversary
R J Reynolds Industries Inc, North Carolina, 1975

Bugler, J and Wakefield, J
The Rise and Triumph of the Universal Cigarette
New Society, May 16, 1968

Corina, M
Trust in Tobacco
Michael Joseph, London, 1975

Davis, A
Package and Print
Faber & Faber, London, 1968

Elliott, R
Brandstand (formerly *Smoke Signals*)
Journal of Cigarette Pack Collectors Association
Massachusetts, 1976 —

Flanagan, R
The Story of Lucky Strike
New York World Fair, 1938

Fortune Magazine
'One out of every Five Cigarettes' (the ten-centers) and 'Spud' (the history of Axton Fisher)
USA, November 1932

Heimann, R H
Tobacco and Americans
McGraw Hill, New York, 1960

Owen Jones
Grammar of Ornament (facsimile edition)
Van Nostrand Reinhold, London and New York, 1972

Lewine, H
Goodbye to All That
McGraw Hill, New York, 1970

Sold American – The First Fifty Years: 1904-1954
American Tobacco Co, New York, 1954

Richard Smith: Paintings 1958-66
Whitechapel Art Gallery, London, 1966

Associations to Join

Cigarette Pack Collectors' Association:
Richard Elliott
61 Searle Street
Georgetown
Massachusetts 01833, USA

In Britain a club for collectors is shortly to be formed by:
Nat Chait
45 High Street
Cranford
Middlesex TW5 9RQ, England

CHAPTER ONE

THE EARLY DAYS OF THE PACK

Cigarette smoking first became a popular and acceptable habit in the 1880s. Within twenty years the tobacco industry found itself one of the major growth areas of the 20th-century economy. The early brands were many in number, magnificent in design, using brilliant colour, lively decoration, strong patterns, with an uninhibited vitality worthy of the early comic books.

The First Cigarette Packs

How, why and when did a human being first take a bit of chopped leaf, wrap it in paper, and, holding it between his lips, set fire to it?

These questions have long exercised the imaginations of the antiquaries of tobacco. Ancient Mexican cigarettes made from corn husks have been found. It is said that Aztec warriors stuffed shredded tobacco into hollow reeds.

In the context of the cigarette as it is understood in this book, a paper tube with a filling of cured tobacco, an early claimant must be the Spanish papalete or cigarillo of about 1700, made by beggars who reconstituted cigar butts.

The first accepted date for the creation of a cigarette factory is 1856 when Robert Gloag started production in London. Many historians have seen this as a response to the habit of cigarette smoking picked up by British troops from Turkish soldiers and Russian prisoners during the Crimean War (1854–1856). However, writing in 1845, Joseph Baker, a tobacconist of Cheapside, London, noted that 'a pinch of Maryland placed within a square piece of paper' was little smoked by the British. The habit was confined to foreign visitors. But by 1851, and perhaps because of the crowds of tourists attracted to the Great Exhibition, there must have been enough trade to satisfy at least two tobacconists, Bacon's of Cambridge, and Simmons of the Burlington Arcade, London, who have records of selling cigarettes during the year.

Virtually no cigarette packing worth note has survived from before the 1880s. Until this date most cigarettes were wrapped in sheets of paper either twisted or glued at the edges. Advertising was probably thought to be much more important, judging by the existence of a small poster for Cope's cigarettes, dated 1877 and showing happy smokers on roller skates. A pack like Richmond's *Virginia Brights*, using the then recently invented hull-and-slide construction, may be said to be the first cigarette pack as we know it. Apart from the early mass-produced brands such as *Woodbines* and *Weights* introduced in the 1880s, Muratti's *Tit-Bits* box must have been one of the earliest British packs (about 1892) to attempt something ambitious.

Before the 1880s most cigarettes were hand-rolled. The industry was transformed virtually overnight by the development of the Bonsack machine, the first cigarette machine to prove workable and efficient. A constantly produced tube of paper-wrapped tobacco was cut by a construction of guillotines into 200 cigarettes at a time, and at under half the cost of the hand-rolled cigarette. In 1885 James Bonsack's invention was bought by James Buchanan Duke, the future creator of the American Tobacco Company. In 1883 it had been purchased by WD & HO Wills, the future nucleus of the Imperial Tobacco Company. Both countries were now equipped for the beginning of a new consumer industry of phenomenal size.

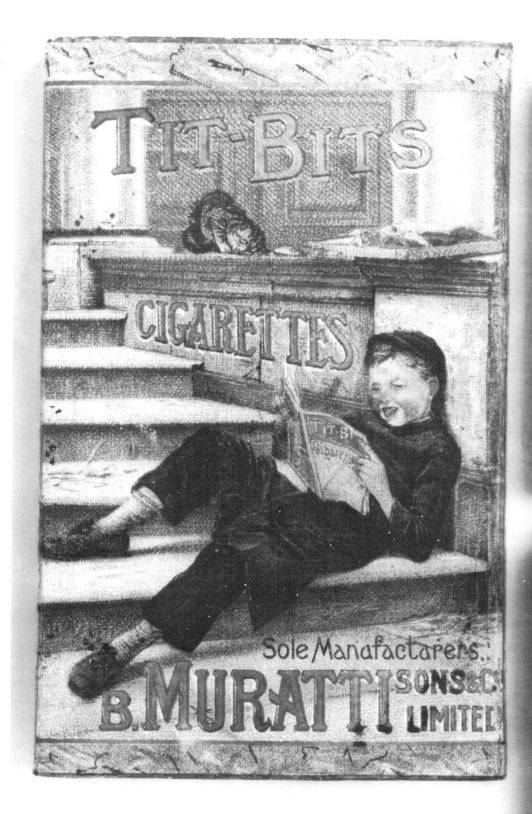

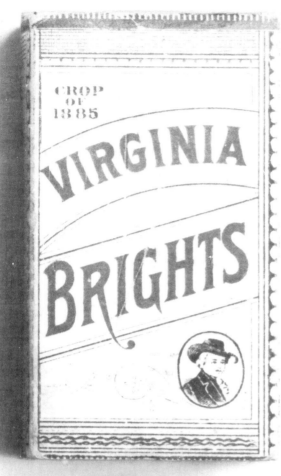

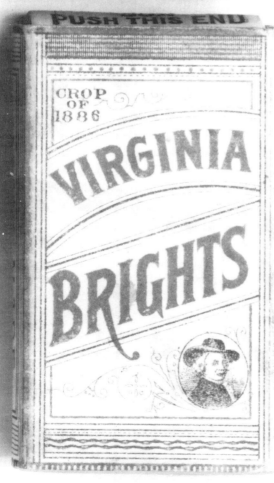

The American Tobacco Company and James 'Buck' Duke

The decision to produce cigarettes rather than smoking or plug tobacco was a brave one, and ultimately a right one. Much of the credit for this farsightedness must go to the dominant figure of James Buchanan 'Buck' Duke (1856–1925), the son of the founder of W Duke Sons & Company, and the man who did not believe that cigarettes were just a passing fad. By 1888, with his improved Bonsack machines he had captured nearly 40% of American production, and, two years later, when he was still only thirty-three, he persuaded his four major rivals, Allen & Ginter, Kinney Tobacco Company, WS Kimball & Company and Goodwin & Company to join him. Together they constituted the American Tobacco Company with a capital of $5 million. The further extension of Duke's interests expanded American Tobacco into what came to be known as the American Trust. Despite the scale of Buck's activities, brands such as those reproduced opposite continued to be sold with no direct control from head office.

Much of the extraordinary success of the American Tobacco Company was due to 'Buck's personality, stubborn persistence, a capacity for taking pains and a streak of cruelty. Duke familiarized himself with all the factory processes and knew all his workers personally. Most importantly for this study, he realized the importance of packaging. The *Virginia Bright* packs on the previous page could well have been mistaken for other products. 'Buck' Duke, (who virtually perfected the hull-and-slide pack), introduced brightly coloured and immediately recognizable images to the fronts of his packs. He is also credited with the invention of the cigarette card. To give some of the cheaper brands wrapped in paper extra protection, a cardboard stiffener was inserted between the rows of cigarettes. Rather than waste a surface, Duke had printed on them advertisements for his products, and then, to encourage the collecting spirit, series of images of famous actresses and athletes. Duke was so pack-minded that he used to count and examine his competitors' packs discarded in the street.

Typical of Duke's house style are the packs shown above, *Cross Cut* (from 1880) and the famous *Cameo* (from 1884), the latter design using the motif

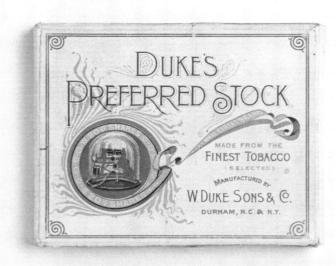

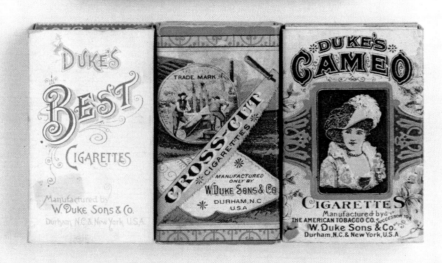

of a cameo ring encircling the pack. *Duke's Best* dates from 1884. Reproduced on the right is a splendid selection of packs produced by the American Tobacco Company and associated firms before 1911.

But already Duke's business manners had caused a lot of opposition from Governmental anti-Trust circles, and from tobacco planters who suspected him of manipulating prices. Roosevelt's administration set in motion moves that were to end in the dissolution of the Trust in 1911. The planters took their own revenge. Masked bands of angry

farmers, calling themselves the Night Riders, rode under cover of dark to destroy Duke's warehouses. In 1901, however, when these disasters were still in the future, Duke had created a virtual tobacco monopoly in the United States. He then turned his eyes to Europe, and specifically to Britain.

In September 1901, Duke, accompanied by his two executives WR Harris and Caleb Dula, landed at Liverpool. At his first meeting with JD and WG Player he is reported to have said, 'Hello boys, I'm Duke from New York come to buy your business.'

The Tobacco War

Whether they were seen as corpulent bloodthirsty bandits, or some of Nature's winners, American industrialists had only just begun to flex their muscles in the European markets by 1900. In May, 1901 the London *Daily Mail* wrote 'At the risk of being thought unpatriotic this journal . . . has persistently called attention to the numberless blows administered to our commercial supremacy, chiefly by reason of the superior educational methods and strenuous life of the American and the German.' In 1903 British industrialists were deeply shocked to discover that while American exports to Britain had risen from £97 million to £127 million during the previous twelve years, British exports to America had fallen by £10 million over the same period. A contemporary cartoon in the *New York Herald* showed the invasion of the American sea monster, marked wheat, cotton, steel and rails, scattering the European powers on the beaches. No

wonder caricatures of Uncle Sam during the year transformed him from the skinny, gaunt old man into a corpulent and complacent figure. The American *Life* magazine published in 1901 some speculations as to what London would eventually look like, 'There is a view of the Royal Exchange surmounted by a gigantic bust of JP Morgan, with the legend *E pluribus unum*, and the corners are surmounted by the American eagle and an American coat-of-arms.' American culture seemed equally threatening. Steamships, castles and the European nobility succumbed to the dollar as London Society danced such dances as the Turkey Trot to new American music. The Union Jack Industries League sponsored in the press an all-British shopping movement, intended to boycott American goods. It is against this background that Duke arrived in England.

'Buck' Duke's Bid for Ogden's

By the end of September, 1901, Duke had made a successful offer of £818,000 for Ogden Ltd, of Liverpool, Wills' main competitor, whose *Guinea Gold* rivalled *Woodbine* in the cheap

range of cigarettes. The Chairman of Ogden's, RH Walters, defending his board's decision, claimed that his firm just could not have competed with the power of the American challenge. He revealed that Duke had set aside £6 million for the invasion of Europe. 'Mr Duke declared that he will secure the Americans the command of the British market in four years or lose £1 million in the enterprise' wrote one newspaper.

In the context of the national obsession with American commercial expansion, the British tobacco industry had long worried about the security of its American leaf supplies. Duke's coup at Ogden's had not found them unprepared. To face the full might of the American Trust, its equivalent, The Imperial Tobacco Company (of Great Britain and Ireland) Limited, was created. The Company was formed in 1901 'to protect British industry, British trade, British methods and British capital, as opposed to American methods and American dollars.' (*Tobacco Trade Review*, 1st October 1901). The Company, with an authorized capital of £15 million, included the leading manufacturers of the day, Wills of Bristol, Player's of

Nottingham, Lambert & Butler of London, Mitchell of Glasgow, Smith of Glasgow, Hignett Brothers of Liverpool, Franklyn, Davey of Bristol, Clarke of Liverpool, Edwards, Ringer & Bigg of Bristol, Richmond Cavendish of Liverpool, Adkin of London, Macdonald of Glasgow and Hignett's Tobacco of London. The company was led by William Henry Wills (1830–1911).

Battle was joined. The Americans cut the price of Ogden's cigarettes. From October 22nd leading American brands were vastly reduced, 10 *Sweet Caporals* from 4½d to 2½d, Duke's *Cameo* from 4½d to 3d and 20 Kinney's *Special* from 11d to 7d. Instead of 1s 10½d 50 Richmond's *Gems* cost 1s 2d. In newspaper advertisements for *Sweet Caporals* the perhaps incredulous public were assured 'A Big Bid for Popularity. In making this reduction no change either in weight, size or quality, has been, or will be effected.'

Forming British-American Tobacco
Duke also went in for saturation coverage in advertising, a level previously unknown in the industry. Imperial responded not with price-cutting, but with a bonus scheme for retailers. Imperial's directors decided that attack was the best form of defence, and were in the process of setting up a company to sell their products in America when both organizations realized that further hostilities would be mutually destructive. The Tobacco War of 1901–1902 was concluded by an agreement whereby each organization agreed to keep off the other's territory. Each acquired trading rights in the other's products. Ogden's was sold to Imperial. And, most importantly of all, Imperial and American Tobacco agreed to set up a new company, British-American Tobacco, registered in Britain to serve both groups' interests in the export markets to the rest of the world. The *Daily Mail* said 'If the Imperial Company has achieved a victory, it will have demonstrated that half the terrors of American competition vanish when it is boldly faced.'

'Buck' Duke had however attracted the unwelcome attentions of the Sherman anti-Trust Commission. Five years of investigation culminated in the decision of the American Supreme Court to dissolve the American Trust 'in restraint of trade and an attempt to monopolize and a monopolization.'

This monumental structure once created there was only one man with the inside knowledge and financial expertise to supervise the demolition, and that was James Buchanan Duke.

The American Tobacco Co was pruned to a smaller size, occupying 37% of the market, and two new companies were created, Liggett & Myers (with a capital of $67 million and about 28% of the market) and Lorillard ($48 million and 15% of the market). The stage was now set for the age of the big brand names, *Camel* and *Lucky Strike*, and the intensive rivalry in advertising that set the pattern for the kind of advertising campaign we know today. The subsequent development of the British tobacco industry took a more gentlemanly course, the spirit of competition between cigarette companies being encouraged by Imperial, but always capable of being moderated if it became too destructive. Some of the splendidly decorative and varied packs in which the British firms were issuing their products when Duke first arrived in Britain, and during the first years of the Imperial Tobacco Company, are shown on the following pages, and are described on page 33.

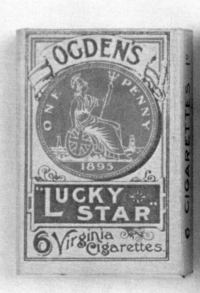

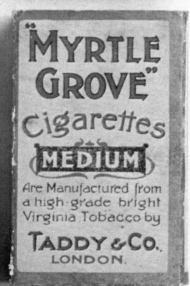

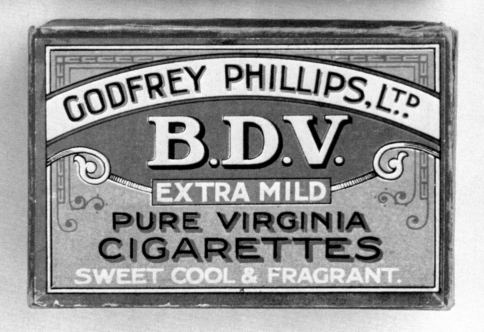

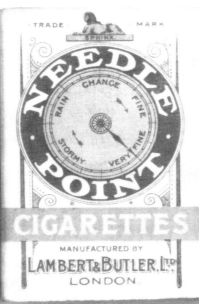

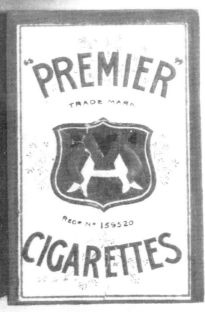

The Best of Early British Pack Design

One of the most striking ways in which the very early (and very beautiful) British packs, shown on pages 30–33, differ radically from modern examples is in their use of humour. *Footprints* (10, Burgin of Castleford, about 1905, page 31) shows Robinson Crusoe poking incredulously at Man Friday's footprints. In a more Music Hall vein, the shambling drunk in *Latch Key* (10, Gulland & Son, Bolton, dated 09, page 32) is trying to unlock a door by its letterbox, oblivious that he is outside a police station. Hardly stunning wit but there is an innocent fun about the packaging that is, of course, impossible today in the age of the anxious, conspicuous consumer. Look at Churchman's *Tenner* (10, dated 15, page 31) having a joke with a ten pound note and the ten pack.

Other brand names touch on areas that will be explored in greater detail later on. The sea and the British Navy are represented by Redford's patriotic *Navy Cut* (10, about 1910, page 31) and by William's *Golden Chain* (10, about 1910, page 32) with its chain frame. Taddy's *Picaroon* (5, about 1905, page 32) evokes the world of the pirate adventurer on the Spanish Main. Contemporary events are also exploited, such as the American Gold Rush in Edwards, Ringer & Bigg's *Klondyke* (10, dated 16, page 30) and there was even the dynamic modern train in Hudden's *Railway Chop* (10, dated 99, page 31). This last pack, with its cigarettes panel hanging from a nail just like a real railway sign, may very well have been an export pack to India since 'Chop' means 'brand or quality' in Anglo-Indian vocabulary.

Flowers and Plants on Packs
Then, as today, a dominant pack theme was the evocation of the Great Outdoors, and particularly, Nature. Of the packs reproduced here, seven have brand names using flowers or growing things, and others, unexpectedly have flowers prominent in the design. The *Burlington* pack from Cohen Weenen (10, about 1905, page 31), despite a name suggesting smart London life, displays a bursting spray of roses. *Musk Rose* (10 perfumed with mouthpieces, Clarke's of Liverpool, about 1910, page 30) and Cope's *Rosebud* (10 gold tipped, about 1910, page 31) also feature roses. Apart from any sexual connotations of the latter name, roses were used to produce an old folk remedy 'Honey of

Roses', used for gargles and lotions to alleviate painful sores in the mouth.

Note also *Sunflower* (Hignett Brothers, 10, dated 05, domestic and exported, page 31), and the delicately woven sprigs of pinks in *Pink of Perfection* (page 30), the cluster of small blue flowers in *Homeland* (Pritchard & Burton, 10, about 1905, page 30). The brand name *Myrtle Grove* (page 30) also evokes plants but is in fact a reference to the house of that pioneer smoker, Sir Walter Raleigh.

Curiously, we also have several brands referring to nuts, *Nutcracker* (Gallaher's, 10, dated 99, page 32) and *Hazel Nut* (Salmon & Gluckstein, page 32). The firms must have heeded the Herbals that suggested that the milk of nut kernels was good for old coughs, and denied that eating nuts led to shortness of breath.

Probably the most sumptuous of the packs of the Great Outdoors was Cope's *Golden Cloud* (10, about 1905, page 31). On the front is a glorious sun-set over the sea, on the back a stream winds slowly to the sea through a deserted rural landscape. It is a considerable achievement in chromolithography, with its subtle blending of colours.

Popular Design Features
Certain design features appear to have been particularly popular at this time, and may well have been accepted as unwritten rules by the artists, who had to draw directly on to the litho stone with the minimum of preparation and in mirror writing. Especially popular is the diagonal sash or row of lettering rising to the right of the pack. Look at the sashes on *Burlington*, *Nutcracker* and *Picaroon* for example, the lettering of *Klondyke* and *Latch Key*.

Many packs derive much of their visual energy from this assymetry, with empty areas filled in by lengths of ribbon. These ribbons, so beloved of the early advertising profession, come in many different shapes and sizes – from thin, nervous stretches caught by the wind in *Klondyke*, to thicker more controlled bands that undulate through the composition, gently turning to and fro, as in *Musk Rose*. In *Homeland* both types appear in the same design. The ribbon at its most confident almost becomes a free-standing panel in Ogden's *Lucky Star* (6 Virginia, featuring a penny from the year of origin, this pack about 1915, page 30).

If plaques, cartouches, ribbons and sashes give the impression of bursting out of the pack, more visual energy is added by the eccentricity of the lettering. The first letter of the brand name very often has a life all of its own. At every opportunity, the 'g' in 'cigarettes' performs its own little dance. The tails of the 'y' and the foot of the 'R' stretch out as if to fill the vacuum around them.

The Lloyd's *Porpoise* pack (20, about 1910, page 32) is really a sort of comic version of the others.

This section ends with two novelty cigarette boxes produced by Kriegsfeld for the Christmas market, beautifully printed and well designed. When the glued card on the top is opened, the lady's leg pops up revealing her petticoats.

These domestic packs certainly contrast sharply with the export packs of the period, often designed for issue by British-American Tobacco, where images, on account of the market they were aimed at, had to be much more simple and obvious.

Brands of the British-American Tobacco Company

Put simply, British-American Tobacco was, and remains, the largest tobacco company in the world. It was created under the agreement signed on the 27th of September 1902 that ended the Tobacco War to deal with the export business of the signatories. Its first chairman was JB Duke, with HH Wills as deputy chairman. With the breaking of the American Trust Duke chose to settle in Britain and continue as chairman of BAT. The company carried Anglo-American brands such as *Woodbine*, *Lucky Strike* and *Sweet Caporal* all over the world (see Introduction). As well as these recognized brands, BAT made and distributed many others intended specifically for areas of mixed languages and dialects. These had to be simple, immediate packs that needed no copy or clever brand names. They relied on visual cyphers for recognition, as shown by Wills' *Scissors*, Wills' *Indian Club*, BAT's *Palm Tree* and *Penknife*.

One sure way of spotting the export pack is the standard phrase, 'The contents of this package are the goods of the successors to . . .' This wording does tend to suggest a product not necessarily connected with either Britain or America, useful in times of political friction.

The pack reproduced opposite, Wills' *Monkey*, is uncharacteristically complex. This example dates from about 1924 but the images seldom change over the years. Wills' *Rough Rider* and Godfrey Phillips' *Torchlight* have survived intact to the present day in overseas markets where pack changes would have meant losses.

Monkey is printed in red and black. Fresh from some medieval bestiary, or perhaps seen in some marginal doodle, the monkey is in the classic 'Hear No Evil' posture, lit by the blaze from the Wills' star trademark. It is importantly a design that makes sense in both directions, an advantage in a non-literate community.

BAT also produced another type of pack – radically different from those with simple images – the exotic wrapper, usually with Eastern trimmings and a Cairo address, attached to the 'banquet box' of cigarettes destined for the coffee table or the sideboard (see the Mavrides wrapper on page 79).

Most of the BAT packs were printed in Britain, and a good proportion by

BRITISH-AMERICAN TOBACCO CO. Ltd.
NEW YORK

Mardon, Son & Hall of Bristol. The few trademark registration books that have survived show extraordinary printing skills, a register that suggests the great tradition of British lithographic printing. Recently increasing freight charges have meant that packaging is now prepared in those countries where the leaf is grown. BAT are thus involved in paper and packing industries throughout the world, and, with the Imperial Tobacco Company, own Mardon Packaging International Ltd, the giant group of firms formed in 1962.

Today BAT have over a hundred tobacco factories in more than fifty countries, and employ over 100,000 people. For the first time since their inception, they have recently developed a brand for the British market, *State Express 555*.

The spirit of BAT is probably best encapsulated by this delightful motif (above) from the cover of a catalogue of about 1920 sent from New York to prospective South American customers. Who could resist the blandishments of this trans-Atlantic man of the world, sleek, poised, faintly amused but of course smoking the firm's product.

Early Packs in Europe

The supremacy of the British and American tobacco industries, and the exporting power of British-American Tobacco, have tended to obscure our knowledge of European tobacco companies. The absence of adequate documentary evidence and the lack of archives in many countries, means an unfocussed background to the development of the industry outside the European State Tobacco monopolies in France and Italy. The preservation of a small group of packs, from which those reproduced on this page are taken, is a major achievement of Niels Ventegodt, whose collection came from Denmark to Britain and is now in the archives of Carreras-Rothman.

Wedding in 1892 of King Christian IX of Denmark (who died in 1896) and Queen Louisa. It is also probably one of the earliest hull-and-slide packs used in Denmark. The pack has been opened here so you can see the clasp of true friendship, rather prim for fifty years of marriage. Notice the two radiating stars of truth and an emblematic figure, very commonly found on these packs, blessing the two cameo portraits with a palm leaf or two.

Symbolic figures can be seen on a pack imported into Denmark from Turkey, *Vivat Fortuna*, an oddly attractive child's version of the Orient. Three little children are framed by an arch previously seen in an illuminated manuscript. One shoots about on a dragon-fly. He represents Turkey. Beneath, two other brothers, Egypt and Greece, frenetically hurl lottery tickets out of a drum, 'Long live Luck'. It is in

for *Job* cigarette papers, which, with minor variations, is the inspiration for the *Lily* pack. Each features the dreamy seductive nymph with full throat, the clinging, muslin robe, drifting ribbons of smoke and even a jewelled knot of hair. The decorative frame of the *Lily* pack, repeated cleverly on the back, is more typical of the heavier Germanic version of Art Nouveau, *Jugendstil*, using sub-Celtic swathes of line, swelling and thinning, accompanied by darting commas on the outside of the frame.

Much less pretentious is the *Tango* cigarette produced in Malta by AG Coussis & Co, and, if the Argentinian Tango was celebrated in Malta at the same time as everywhere else, dating from about 1912. In an age dominated by the two giants of tobacco manufacture, their mutual hostility, reconciliation, and the birth of an even more gigantic offspring, perhaps it is fitting to end the chapter with this unpretentious naive pack, filled with open-eyed innocence and wonderment at the latest dance craze from the Americas, the Society Tango. From 1910 onwards the Tango was synonymous with fast, racy living – the participants danced in sudden smouldering rushes, practically cheek to cheek. The Maltese dancers keep a respectable distance (the close grasp of the hands is quite beyond the designer), but the pack must have carried that air of fashionable naughtiness.

Soon, however, the sensations of the day – Cubist art, the Tango Tea, Diaghalev and the Russian Ballet amongst them – were to be swept away by the privations, the destruction and social upheaval caused by the Great War.

From the insufficient evidence available, European packs before 1918 seem to have projected a much more aristocratic image than British cigarettes, as shown for example by the Dutch pack *Kroning's Sigarreten* featuring the Queen's head, and the German *Fursten* pack bearing a portrait of Karl, Prince von Schweden-Norwegen.

One of the rarest European packs in the Ventegodt collection is the *Jubilaum* cigarette, commemorating the Golden

fact a lottery cigarette pack, 'La Compagnie de Cigarettes de Loterie', the rules of which are printed in Danish on the reverse of the pack.

The *Lily* pack, made by Przedecki of Breslau in about 1910, is one of the few to show the least interest in Art Nouveau. Bearing in mind the potential for pin-ups, curling smoke and decorative surfaces, this absence of the style is surprising. The most celebrated link between Art Nouveau imagery and smoking is Alphonse Mucha's poster

CHAPTER TWO

THE GREAT WAR AND BEYOND

Cigarette smoking was, from the turn of the century, associated with the manly vigour of the fighting forces. This was further emphasized by the popularity of the habit among soldiers on the battlefields. By 1919, more tobacco was smoked in cigarettes than in pipes. Pack design took on a new elegance and a frivolity suitable to the post-war mood of the Twenties.

The First World War

The martial spirit is certainly shown in the three packs illustrated at the beginning of this chapter on page 37. Martin's *Glory Boys* (UK, about 1910) shows a notable act of heroism by a soldier who is suitably decorated on the reverse of the pack. The *Old Glory* cigarette (Shanghai, about 1920) features the Stars and Stripes, and Lusby's *Iron Duke* (UK, about 1905) shows the Duke of Wellington, perhaps at Waterloo. The fine qualities of the original materials, the subtlety of the printing, were in fact only really possible during times of peace, or during a war such as the Boer War which did not cause economic disruption. Only under such circumstances could cigarette packs be well prepared visual propaganda.

In Britain the most damaging initial effect of the outbreak of the Great War was suffered by Wills, who, in deference to their French allies, were forced to pulp a 'Waterloo' series of cigarette cards. Another series, 'Musical Celebrities', was immediately purged of Germanic composers. By 1917 cigarette cards had been discontinued. Packaging economies included limited colour printing, cheaper finishing processes and the substitution of paper for board. In Britain a Tobacco Control Board was set up to regulate supplies. Gradually advertising shrank, and British cigarette production devoted itself to supplying troops at the Front.

The pressures on supplies in America were equally great. Heimann in *Tobacco and Americans*, reproduces a photograph of a line of freight cars carrying Bull Durham Roll Your Own tobacco for shipment to Europe. Each car carries a rousing slogan, 'Smoking out the Kaiser', 'Over the Top with Eleven Million sacks of Bull's'. One car added, 'And this is only one half of each month's shipment'. In 1918 the complete year's production of the Bull Durham factory was requisitioned by the Government.

Private organizations also sent cigarettes to the troops. The 'Our Boys in France Tobacco Fund' of Philadelphia existed for this purpose, '25 cents keeps a fighting man happy for a week'. The Fund passed the donor's name to the soldier or sailor who, if he had time, expressed his gratitude. The Fund thundered, 'The Anzacs have all the tobacco they can use . . . The French *poilus* never want for a smoke – their friends are on the job.' Some of the cigarettes sent out by the Funds were decorated with patriotic images, and perhaps this was the genesis of *The Allies* pack, keeping the world safe for Democracy by shutting the safe on the Kaiser.

In Britain similar schemes operated both inside and outside the tobacco companies. Wills' employees ran their own schemes but the firm offered many types of orders at specially reduced prices for 'our fighting boys'. For 2s 6d you could get Order A sent to your son or sweetheart, 250 Woodbines and a tinder lighter. For an extra sixpence you could treat him to the same order with an added $\frac{1}{2}$lb of *United Service* smoking tobacco. The YMCA in both Britain and America sent thousands of these stamped packs to the troops.

Woodbine and *Black Cat* were particularly associated with war-time smoking. The Rev GA Studdert-Kennedy, one army padre who was particularly generous with his cigarettes on tours round the trenches, was known as 'Woodbine Willy', after a popular Music Hall song of the turn of the century. Carreras sent off free cigarettes for the troops with pocket dictionaries and phrase books, their Black Cat trademark making several appearances in political cartoons of the period.

Like the other arts, the art of the cigarette pack did not exactly flourish in conditions of total War. Significantly, the two most familiar images were marketed on packs brought out after the war, Gerard's *Fighter* (UK, about 1925) and the Danish brand *Tommy Atkins* (about 1930).

Quoth the Raven

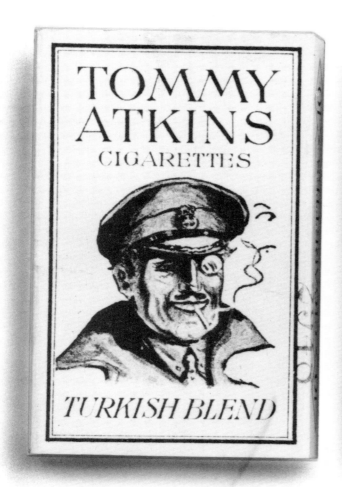

Military Might

That the smoking of cigarettes is associated with the Armed Forces comes as no surprise – a good excuse for combining marketing with patriotism and national resolve. For the pack artist it provides a splendid opportunity for colour, dash and daring on the pack front. Archer's *Zouave* (UK, about 1910) represents everything you could expect from the foreign soldier. Here, the Zouave, a soldier in a French regiment originally raised in Algeria, and at one time recruited from

bravery (again perhaps not the associations wanted by today's cigarette manufacturers). On the front of the pack a Life Guard on horseback flourishes his sword, his plume blowing in the wind. On the back the artist has shown arguably the most celebrated military event in British military history, the Battle of Balaclava when the Light Brigade charged the Russian guns as a result of misunderstood orders and were decimated in their devotion to duty, their refusal to disobey that order. The Charge as shown on the pack is so frantic that the horses give the illusion of bursting over the panel bearing the maker's name, and attacking the smoker.

the markets with literally hundreds of brands that asserted the power of land and sea forces. The packs shown here are only a tiny proportion of what was actually produced.

During the period that packs concentrated most on this kind of imagery there was, in Britain, a pervading unease at the respective armament levels of the great World powers, and at the capacity of British forces to resist Germany's challenge to the Empire. Two brands from the period (not shown here), Cope's *Man of War* and Lambert & Butler's *Gunboat*, carried the message of nautical supremacy not only to the anxious home market but also to the rest of the world. The emphasis on military might on export packs seems to have been quite deliberate. Wills' *Fearless* was exported throughout the world, to Africa, India and Asia. The pack front shows the last defiant group of British soldiers gathering round the flag, facing the rushing hoards of Zulu warriors, with their resolve and revolvers. Fearless cigarettes smoked by fearless men. This Imperial scene may have the appearance of a wood engraving in one of the cheap illustrated newspapers but it did carry surreptitiously into every pocket a powerful image of British power.

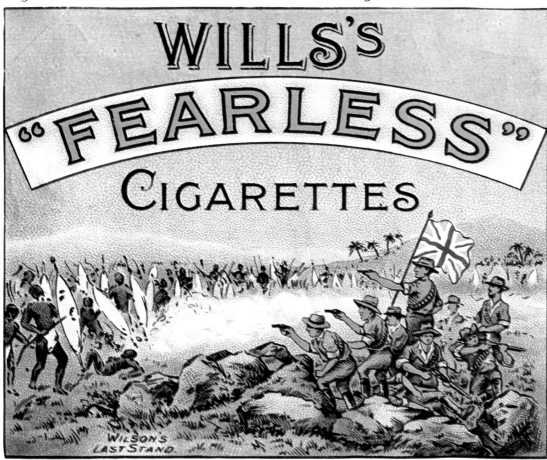

WILSON'S LAST STAND.

the Berbers, stares rapaciously out at his customers with his straggly moustache and close-cropped hair. The brand name may even have been chosen to get a bit of North African exotica onto the pack, particularly the famous picturesque costume the Zouaves wore. It is interesting that the Zouaves fought for the first time outside Algeria in the Crimean War, when British and French soldiers are meant to have adopted the habit of smoking.

The Crimean War is perhaps also a secondary theme in that personification of British military might, the *Life Guard*, (UK, about 1900). The name today seems to have acquired overtones of cleanliness and hygiene, but then it rang with heroic endeavour and foolhardy

National Military Images
It is interesting that policemen, farmers, or indeed design historians have not been celebrated in a similarly enthusiastic way on cigarette packs. Throughout the world from Angola to China, from Bangladesh to Bolivia, emblems of national military might figure prominently in designs, reminding us of the constant propaganda value of the pack, on the smoker's person or at least within easy reach twenty-four hours a day, and flourished as many times as its cigarettes. Smoking became a mass habit in the twenty years before the First World War. During this period both American and European packs used martial images but it was the British tobacco companies who flooded

Cigarette Packs and the Army
There may have been a deeper and less exalted reason for associating cigarettes with, say, the Army, as in Smith's *Forage Cap* (UK, about 1913). In a Government Committee report on the Physical Deterioration of the population (London, 1904), an Inspector of Schools noted that there had been a drastic deterioration in the standards of Army recruiting material. To the usual list of causes, alcohol, poverty and idleness, many voices added that of the curse of the burning weed. The strength of the Anti-Smoking lobby in the first years of the twentieth century has been largely overlooked. While society ladies demonstrated their contempt, boxers, stage personalities and politicians inveighed against 'the vice'. Baden Powell, the heroic defender of Mafeking during the Boer War, and founder of the Scout movement, had no doubts about the matter, 'when a lad smokes before he is fully grown up, it is almost sure to make his heart feeble. Any Scout knows that smoking spoils his eyesight and also his sense of smell which is of the greatest importance to him for scouting on active service.'

Yet cigarette manufacturers, remember, had found themselves at the turn of the century, involved in one of

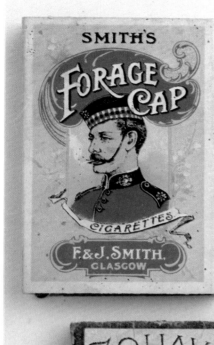

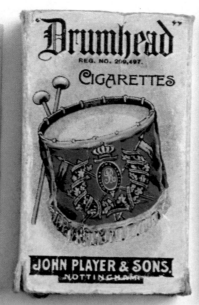

the most remarkable growth industries seen since the days of the early Industrial Revolution. Faced with this challenge they had to use every device known to the advertising profession. What held for sporting packs (see pages 84–85) held also for military packs.

British Packs in the Boer War
We first see military images used extensively on British packs during the Boer War in South Africa (1899–1902). In 1901 Ogden's advertised their *Guinea Gold* cigarettes by juxtaposing the pack and Lord Roberts, the commander of the British Army in South Africa. His dour features were also used to inspire the smoker on Wills' *United Services* (about 1905). On the back of this pack is another all-action

scene of a gun-crew firing at the enemy. When Roberts was succeeded by Kitchener, Ogden's featured their *Guinea Gold*, ('Always wanted when there', with the new chief 'Always there when wanted'). Ogden's even began to use large cartoons of the Boer leader Paul Kruger. This series of very funny drawings, reproduced in the British press, shows him finding solace with a quick puff on a *Guinea Gold*, or, more suitable to the British mood, stealing crates of the product. During the Boer War cigarette sales were used, presumably for the first time, as a charitable exercise by one manufacturer, Hersey of London, who sold *The Old Flag* virginia cigarettes for the benefit of the 'Soldiers' and Sailors' Families' Association' with the slogan, 'To keep the home that Tommy left behind him'.

This background may go some way to explain the volume of Edwardian military imagery – the uninhibited display of Nathan's *British Heroes* (about 1905), its stalwarts flanking the national emblems, the call to arms of Player's *Drumhead* (about 1910) and the heroic ideal of Smith's *Forage Cap*. One of the most impressive of this type of pack is Lusby's *Iron Duke*, a rare pack (about 1905) showing the Duke of Wellington carefully picking his way across the battlefield, perhaps Waterloo. The lettering is eccentric, almost in cartoon style, arranged in a florid, vulgar cartouche. The joviality of the letters with their rounded, almost melting qualities, is common to many packs of the period. From behind the Duke's head, comes the clarion call 'Up Guards and at 'em'.

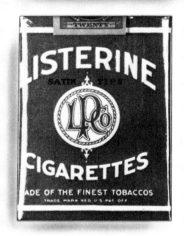

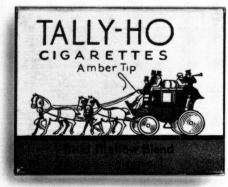

Pack Art in the Twenties

Once supplies and packaging returned to normal, the 1920s was really a decade of 'Battling Big Brands'. In America, *Camel*, *Lucky Strike* and *Chesterfield*, in Britain, Player's *Medium* and *Weights*, Wills *Woodbine* and *Gold Flake*, Carreras *Black Cat* and *Craven A*, fought out carefully considered campaigns for market supremacy. Reproduced on this page are three new brands introduced in the 1920s, – Wills' *Flag* (1926), Wills' *Star* (1923) and

emblem tactfully blotted out to mollify outraged smokers at some time when anti-British feeling ran high.

Wills' *Star*, a new small cigarette, (of localized appeal in Britain, but widely exported), came out in 1923, using a white star with gold trimmings on a dark blue ground, a variation on Wills' well-known trademark. Shown here is a typical tin label used for export. Neither *Flag* nor *Star* have complicated names, no finesse is needed for blending colour into colour. Simplicity, visual immediacy and balance are the key factors.

Godfrey Phillips' *Army Club* was one of the successful new brands. It was

the graphic flourishes of Scotten Dillon's *Yankee Girl* (about 1922) contrasting with the *Marlboro* pack introduced in 1925. Axton Fisher's *Clown* (1921–1924) and Brown & Williamson's *Go* (1920) are splendid bits of design extravagance, the creation of an almost primitive style. *Clown* may also be seen as a rude gesture to American Tobacco's *Lucky Strike*, a girl dressed as a clown sticks her head through the familiar bull's eye.

Two novel packs relevant to the later debate on smoking and health came out in the Twenties, *Listerine* cigarettes (1927, impregnated with antiseptic oils), and, less comfortably, Batt

Godfrey Phillips' *Army Club* (1924) together with *Senior Service*, one of the big sellers of the decade, particularly as an export to Canada. Changes to the Edwardian designs of the established brands were minimal, but these three brands show a spareness and economy of design characteristic of a new age. The *Flag* design on the pack (dated 1927) has refused all panels, ribbons and excess decoration. The central silhouette is of a pale blue battleship, framed by two thin blue lines that go all the way round the packet. Only the Union Jack and the red disc are allowed opaque colour. The export version of the brand, here made in Egypt, has its offending British

heavily advertised in the Press and particularly associated with a large neon sign in London. Spectacular advertising was a feature of the Twenties, a product of the development of the propaganda techniques of the First World War. One brand launched in America in 1926, Lorillard's *Old Gold*, used comic strips in press advertisements and exploited the new idea of the Blindfold Test. The *Old Gold* Aeroplane, 'The Voice of the Sky', broadcast live piano music and commercial breaks over American cities in 1927. Something of the brash exuberance is reflected in the packs of the period, the exotic richness of Khoury's *El Ahram* (1925, Egypt greets America),

Brothers' *Wooden Kimona Nails* (1923), its verse on the back challenging, 'Stop here a moment and cast an eye/ As you were once so once was I/ As I am now so you will be/ Smoke up before you follow me.'

In few of the American packs is there any firm interest in the abstract and geometrical. There is a surviving fascination with imagery on packs, most of it amusing, if not exactly hysterically funny. To close this chapter overleaf are two elegant and imaginative designs for box wrappers, which probably date from this period, *The Blue Horse Pills* and *Bonnell Blend*, both beautifully drawn, sensitively coloured and as charming as packs can be.

BONNELL BLEND

CHAPTER THREE

CLASSIC PACKS 1

Throughout the world there have been certain brands that have survived and prospered to become synonymous with the smoking of cigarettes – *Lucky Strike, Camel, Raleigh, Chesterfield* and *Marlboro* in America, *Black Cat* and *Woodbine* in Britain. The pack fronts are immediately recognizable. To this Hall of Fame is promoted the exuberant Bolivian, *La Habanera*.

The Face on the Pack

Many of the brands shown in this book have been going for seventy years, and in some cases are nearing their centennials. Changing fashions can be seen both in the overall design of the pack, and also in the way the brand characters have been altered. Two well-known packs, *Raleigh* (USA) and *Black Cat* (UK), illustrate these changes well.

Raleigh

As you might expect from such a versatile man, celebrated poet, explorer, lover, and tobacco grower, Sir Walter Raleigh presents himself in many moods and guises on the various *Raleigh* pack designs issued over the years. On an undated slide for 5 cigarettes, probably complimentary, he is very much the historical figure, in a primitive linear style that looks as if it has been taken from an engraving. In the second pack, (about 1935), he has acquired a coat of arms and a cartouche afflicted with severe decay at the edges. The full magnificence of his court doublet is now revealed – it was Raleigh after all who supposedly introduced tobacco into the court of Queen Elizabeth I. In the third pack, of about 1940, that certain woodenness has been replaced by the glow of human warmth. An apparent operation on his nose has given him a lean and hungry look and his moustache is that of the man about town, not the bar room heavy. He is now ready for more romantic roles.

In the *Raleigh* 903 tipped cigarette pack of 1947, Sir Walter had had a face-lift and change of clothes suitable to his reputation as a poet – the gaunt, wary, even cynical face manages to muster something like a watery smile. The brow is so much more expressive than before. The hat is balanced, the ruff fluffed up, and, perhaps because it distracted before, the cartouche, a sort of pirate's map, has been simplified.

At last, here is Raleigh (plain end) with the debonair air of the lover, the half smile playing across his face, which after some weeks spent away from court, has become more refined, boyish, smooth. Unfortunately, in the process he has lost his body, his armorial bearings and cartouche. Released from the confines of the frame, his head floats slowly across the white ground, the extended feather sticking jauntily out from the hat. Alas, but poor Sir Walter encountered the

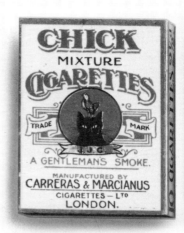

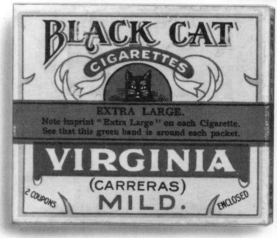

stripe designers of the 1960s and in his disembodied form, he is kept now in a stout red box on the front of *Raleigh Filter Kings*.

Black Cat

Carreras' *Black Cat* did not enjoy the range of emotions permitted to the talented Sir Walter, but what he lacks in expressive power, he made up in sheer application as a public celebrity. He didn't represent one brand – he represented the firm, and in one shape or other can be found on *Chick*, *Black Cat*, *Craven A* and *Black Cat No 9* (son of *Black Cat*).

Although of course a symbol of good luck, there actually was a black cat in Carreras' Wardour Street premises. Customers called the shop there the 'Black Cat Shop' so the name came to be closely associated with the firm and included on early packaging. The gateway of the firm's famous Arcadia works was even flanked by two monumental statues of the creature, just to remind the workers who was Boss.

Although only partly seen on the pack, the Black Cat adopted a more defiant full length pose on early advertisements, a latter day Puss in Boots, who 'defied competition' with flag and sword during the First World War. Carreras' early campaigns featuring the cat set standards in both ingenuity and dottiness. The Black Cat ran his own Great Black Cat Football competition, and in 1913 organized the 'money for packs' Black Cat Day. You could get his party games, even a fancy dress costume, and on occasion he made his representatives dress up as cats.

His portrait on the early *Chick* (10, about 1910) is given minimal detail, two slit eyes and black spiky whiskers. He is even made to suffer the indignity of a chick on the head. On the *Black Cat* pack (about 1915, green brand for extra large cigarettes), he has an alert and perky look, rather like the cartoon character Felix the Cat. The ebullient lettering – note the trumpetting 'A's' – the ornate background, changed year after year, almost pack by pack. In the Twenties the cartoon version stayed on the back while a pin-up photo, set in heavy metal, graced the front. After the end of coupon trading, the design was stripped to a mere porthole and handle supporting the cat. The brand made a comeback as *Black Cat No 9* interestingly reviving the old Felix face. To complete the picture Carreras' ultimate good luck pack *Three Cats* has been added as well as an interesting German version where the cat seems to have taken to 'the habit' himself.

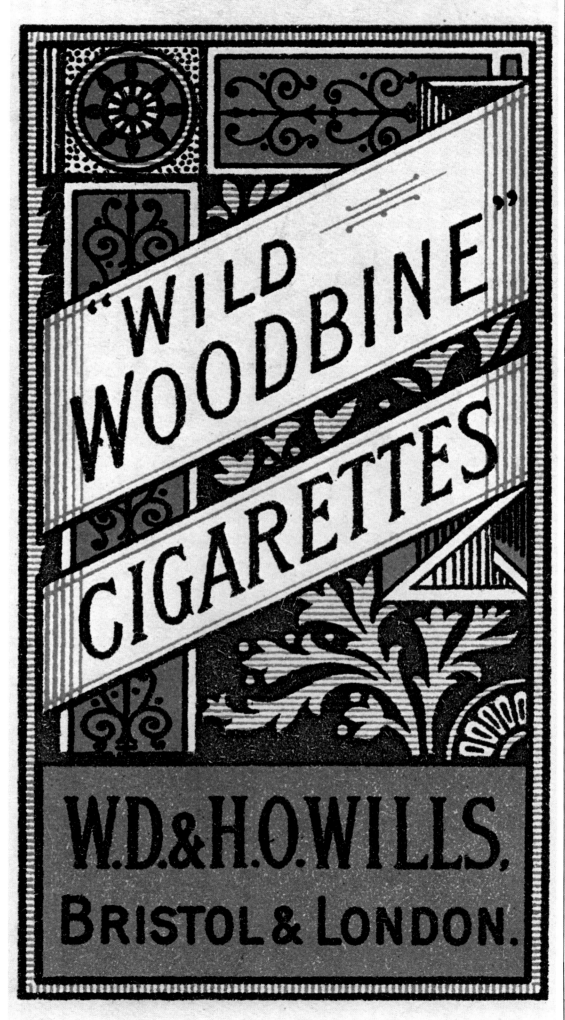

Wills' Wild Woodbine

Wild Woodbine, the People's cigarette was launched in Britain, along with a companion brand, *Cinderella* (shown opposite), – Wills liked to hedge their bets – in 1888 at a penny for five. The original *Woodbine* packet was a strip of paper folded around five cigarettes with only the doubled layer of the glued edge to add strength; it was not until the 1930s that cigarette cards, or stiffeners, were put into the paper 5. Many people still have treasured memories of the rituals involved in getting 5 *Woods* from a vending machine.

The name *Wild Woodbine* had originally been used for a relatively minor brand of smoking tobacco for export. The brand was the first of the mass-produced, low priced cigarettes manufactured on the new Bonsack machines bought by Wills from James Bonsack. Machine-made cigarettes, although mistrusted at first by a public who seemed to prefer the crude, variable hand-made varieties, were neater in appearance, easier to smoke, and more economic in the use of materials. For cost and speed of production, the Bonsack machine was the only possible future development for Wills. In 1891 over 53 million *Woodbines* were produced. Two years later this output had trebled. The price stayed at a penny for 5 until 1915, when a farthing was added. By February 1920, 5 cost 2d, a price sustained until 1939. Packs of 10 were introduced in 1916, and 20 in 1930, although the old pack of 5 was still available in 1973.

But why *Wild Woodbine*? The brand name suggests natural things, while the name of the sister brand *Cinderella* has undertones of the poor relation, who finally makes good, a theme made quite clear in showcards and counter cards. But is it possible that *Woodbine* is using more complex associations, tapping the last memories of folk medicine?

Culpeper's Complete Herbal and English Physician enlarged, published in London in 1823, says of the Woodbine plant: 'It is a plant so common, that every one that hath eyes knows it . . . Dr Reason hath taught the common people to use the leaves or flowers of this plant in mouth water: and by long continuance of time, hath so grounded it in the brains of the vulgar.' The plant was 'of Mercury and appropriated to the lungs.'

Wild Woodbine's Competitors

If all this sounds a bit too fanciful, then it is possible that the original brand name was inspired by one of the many references to the plant in English literature. Shakespeare writes of the Bower of Titania 'quite over-canopied with luscious Woodbine' in *Midsummer Night's Dream*. The poet Shirley wrote richly of the 'Honey-dropping Woodbine'. In most evocations of the Rustic Bower, the plant is synonymous with unalloyed gratification of the senses, but pure and unsullied. 'To deck the wall, or weave the bower/The Woodbines mix in am'rous play/And breathe their fragrant lives away', wrote Cotton. So much has the name *Woodbine* come to be associated with cheap cigarettes that it is difficult to take these lines as they were intended.

next seventy years or so it constantly threatened *Woodbine's* position as brand leader but never quite consolidated its gains. In 1897 the Ulster tobacco manufacturer Thomas Gallaher began to market his own response to the *Woodbine*, *Park Drive* cigarettes. There was another variant that cigarette manufacturers had to cater for – regional preference. In the cheaper range, *Park Drive* sold well in the Midlands, while *Weights* were more popular in the South East of England.

The *Woodbine Red Label* brand, incorporating a certain amount of the cheaper Commonwealth leaf, was introduced in May, 1939, after the price of *Woodbine* had gone up for the first time in nineteen years. The *Red Label* brand was intended for sale at the old price in vending machines, but did not catch on and was withdrawn in November 1942, when prices had to go up again.

porary richness of decoration, but on closer examination that decoration is primarily geometric – wheel and fan shapes, pseudo-Renaissance mouldings on rectangular panels. The ribbon itself does not contort and curve away into space. It follows the usual upwards diagonal across the face of the pack, and then is turned back upon itself in sharp, angular forms. The surfaces here imitate metal rather than silk or paper, and are much more suitable to the brand's clientele. This was no scented creature of the boudoir, or elegant smoke for the toff. The mechanical hatching at the ends of the ribbon emphasize this quality.

The design philosophy that is at the root of *Woodbine*, and which can be felt on so many other patterns for packaging in the 1870s and 1880s, is that of Christopher Dresser, the botanist and designer whose book *The Principles of Decorative Design*, published in 1873, illustrates several related shapes and patterns.

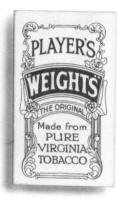

The original design reproduced opposite was probably the most celebrated of the abstract packs of its day. It has a richness of imagery just as great as, say, Pritchard & Burton's *Homeland*, or Cohen Weenen's *Burlington*. The difference between our reactions to these packs is of course governed by the fact that *Woodbine* was an extremely successful brand, the pack seen everywhere, while *Burlington* did not for long survive the frantic competition of the market before 1914.

The success of *Woodbine* prompted Player's to produce their Player's *Weights* cigarette in May 1889, when it was first called Player's *No 1 Virginia*. It was originally sold loose from a cabinet, weighed to the customer's order and then sealed in an envelope printed with a blue decoration. Perhaps it was the way in which these cigarettes were ordered that led Player's to market it as Player's *Weights*. Over the

Details in Design

All three brands that dominated the cheaper range had ornate packets that remained largely unchanged until the post-1950 streamlining of pack design. Comparing the design of *Woodbine* with others of the period before 1914, it can be seen how geometric, even severe is the *Woodbine* pack. The original lettering shows little of the flourish and fun of such packs as Lloyd's *Porpoise* (page 32). The forms are clean and eminently readable, as is the basic structure of the pack. For a front that uses the theme of nature, it is surprisingly free from vegetation and tendrils. The woodbine plant itself appears in a highly abstracted, inaccurate and spiky form, as a decorative infill behind the ribbons and panels. *Woodbine* has been introduced as the People's cigarette, and throughout its history it has always taken a no-nonsense attitude to packaging and advertising. It did adopt the contem-

Competing Brands

The Player's *Weights* pack design seems to have been copied exactly from the old envelopes in which the cigarettes were sold by weight. It is not so radical a design as *Woodbine*. The brand name is immediately readable, thrown forward from a dark background, although the designer could not resist the Baroque details and subtle clusters of roses that, by association, breathe fragrant perfume over the pack.

Gallaher's *Park Drive* is perhaps the most anarchic of the three. As if the ribbons, strings and sashes were seen having too much fun, the gyrations and the swellings of the letters too extrovert in behaviour, a large straight band is lowered down both sides, restoring a sort of order.

All these designs proved too rich for the public's palate after 1950. First to go from *Woodbine* were the inverted commas, and then the 'Wild' was removed. The pack front had become a mere panel on the face of the pale green front. By 1966 all that was left of the original design was a sprig of vegetation on two flat colour stripes (see pages 122–123).

As is mentioned in the Introduction, famous packs breed rumours. *Woodbine* is no exception. Years ago it was said that the design of the pack front, far from being an abstract arrangement, related to a peculiarly strange story about a Japanese gentleman and a fan. Sadly there appears to be no-one alive today who can complete the story.

The Camel Story

In 1913 the American public were teased in newspapers and on billboards with the bare slogan, 'The Camels are Coming'. Appetites were further whetted by the legend, 'Camels! Tomorrow there will be more Camels in this town than in all Asia and Africa combined.' The mystery was revealed when RJ Reynolds' Tobacco Company unveiled their *Camel* cigarette.

An itinerant tobacco merchant, RJ Reynolds had opened a plant for plug tobacco in Winston, North Carolina in 1875, producing such brands as *Old Rip*, *Fat Back*, *Red Meat*, *Wine Sap*, and (surprisingly polysyllabic) *Minnie Ogburn*. Growth of the plug business in Winston was so enormous that by 1897 the town was calling itself 'The

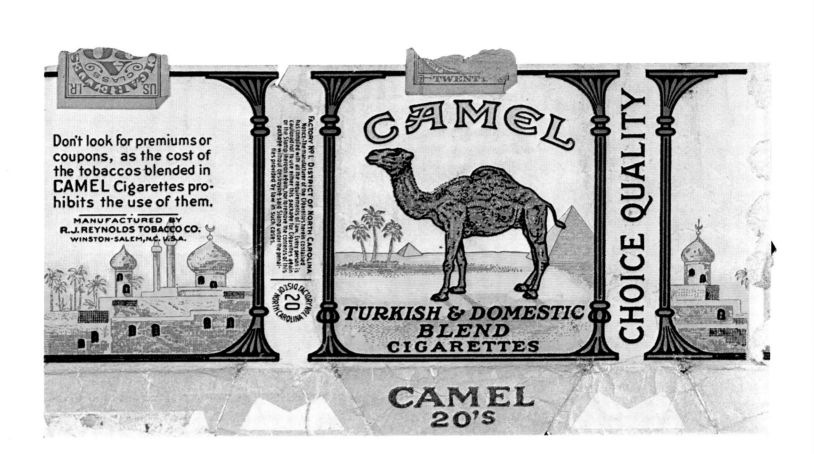

Storm Centre of the Plug Industry', and was the third largest centre of tobacco manufacturing. Reynolds was too successful to avoid the attentions of 'Buck' Duke. Faced with 'War' or 'Merger' he chose the latter.

In 1907 Reynolds launched a pipe tobacco called *Prince Albert*, featuring a very flattering portrait of Edward VII on the package. The brand was a blend of burley (flue cured) and bright (air cured) tobaccos, and proved a great success.

Based on this blend, *Camel* appeared in a blaze of publicity. For a quarter of a million dollars the brand launch was undertaken by one of the leading advertising agencies of the day, NW Ayer & Son, who had won their spurs on the Prince Albert campaign, 'The pipe tobacco that can't bite your tongue'. Sales in 1914 reached 425 million cigarettes, and such was the national appeal that, by 1921, this figure had reached 30 billion annually. The pack, which has hardly changed since 1913, has both proved itself extremely successful in visual impact and practica-

bility, and also become synonymous with American smoking for generations of people outside the United States.

'Over the years, the *Camel* pack has acquired a mystique of its own,' writes Jerome Beatty in the Reynolds Centenary booklet. 'People saw images – a woman, a lion and so forth – in the illustration of Old Joe the camel. Others liked to demonstrate how the word CHOICE reads the same in the mirror as it does on the label. There were all manner of parlor and bar games. Count the ''e's'' or ''t's'' on the back panel. Count the Camels (there's one behind the pyramid). Clever people have been making a variety of objects out of empty packages – from ashtrays to picture frames to potholders. The package had even attained a kind of spiritual honor when a United States Congressman, at an audience with the Pope, accidentally held a pack of *Camels* along with some medals as they were blessed by the Pope.'

The individuality of the *Camel* pack can be emphasized by comparing it with another brand in the Reynolds'

family, *Red Kamel*, a cork tipped Turkish cigarette, 10 for 10 cents, and originally introduced by the Import Tobacco Manufacturing Company in 1908. The Turkish cigarette box is so obviously a design of its time, the Middle Eastern city in the trees, the camel and its handler sprinting across the square watched by a group of contented Arabs. The lettering of the brand name is exuberant, to say the least. The 'R' even reaches out for the 'Kamel'. The original design for the *Camel* pack is, on the other hand, a masterpiece of simplicity, lettering constrained within its band of space, with a sobriety more appropriate to a Turkish/domestic blend.

The design was so much a part of people's lives that, in 1958, when the company decided to tidy up the pack by shifting the pyramid that underpinned the camel's rump to the far distance, 'several tons of angry mail' protested at this radical interference in the nation's inheritance. The firm capitulated. Even the eccentric 'A' and gout-footed 'L' returned intact.

The Camel and its Imitators

In the planning stage of the Camel cigarette Reynolds produced two pilot labels, for *Kamel* and *Camel*. The latter name was chosen perhaps to help distinguish it from *Red Kamel*. The prototype pack showed a ludicrous camel with goitrous neck and cloven hoofs, drawn probably from memory. But already the two pyramids, the group of palm trees and the oasis at the back of the pack were established as design features. All Reynolds needed now was a persuasive looking camel, or rather dromedary.

Luckily, by chance the world famous Barnum & Bailey Circus was touring near Winston and, so the legend goes, RC Haberkern, a Reynolds' employee, persuaded them to allow their dromedary, known as 'Old Joe', to be photographed for use on the pack design. Old Joe would not keep still for his

photograph, so his trainer, as formidable a figure as the beast, whacked him on the nose with a stick. Outraged, Old Joe pulled back his ears, raised his tail, and adopted a posture halfway between offended dignity and aggression. As you can see from the original photograph taken at some time during this episode, the stance and features of the original dromedary, shorn of the bridle, were reproduced exactly for the pack design, against a background possibly derived from the reverse of the *Murad* pack (see Introduction).

What distinguishes the design is the restricted colour range of dark reds and browns used for camel and frame on a field of pale colour. Its simplicity must have contrasted strongly with the exotic packs of the day. The edges of the soft pack are accentuated with twin columns that have bulbous capitals and bases which round off the corners of the pack. On the back is the silhouette of the Middle Eastern city that is found on so many Turkish packs, minarets and domes on the skyline. Apart from sug-

gesting the oasis in the desert, the zone of sky provides a field for the slogan, 'Don't look for premiums or coupons, as the cost of the tobaccos blended in CAMEL cigarettes prohibits the use of them'. This makes clear that *Camel* is not a gift brand, unlike many which offered coupons for gifts – bootlaces, pencils, garters and the like.

Animal Imitators

Such a successful brand is bound to have its imitators. *Camel* was one of many American brands using Middle Eastern imagery after 1910 (see page 117), but the classic simplicity of the design, the animal set in profile against the distant view of landscape, all framed in that characteristic way, has influenced many brands all over the world. How closely these imitators approached the original can be seen from *Emu*, here made by a Costa Rican firm but a brand owned by British-American Tobacco. Also mobilized for active service on the pack is the Stag at Bay, in *Monroe* (Brazil) with a blend of Turkish and

Indian buildings at the back, and the horse in *Derby* (Paraguay) – more like donkey but there is at least a racetrack behind. The *Giraffe* pack, made by the Sincere Tobacco Company of Malaysia, is the most delightful of these variations on a theme. On the back, the copy reads 'The pure tobacco is then performed (sic) by special process, for these reasons the cigarettes are absolutely harmless to the throat . . .' a point perhaps emphasized by the choice of a giraffe as brand animal.

The use of pyramid imagery in pack art is mentioned on page 78, but at least three packs show some passing acquaintanceship with the *Camel*, Petteroe's *Kamel* (Norway), Fok Hing's *Camel Rider* (Malaysia), and the African Cigarette Company's *Pall Mall*, rising inappropriately over the Pyramids. The Danish import pack *Canada* provides a bizarre juxta-position.

Great Brand Rivalries

The very success of Reynolds' *Camel*, its Turkish and American blend, immediately stung other competitors into a response. Liggett & Myers up-dated a brand called *Chesterfield*. In 1917, the American Tobacco Company's *Lucky Strike* entered the field. Turkish cigarettes and all domestic cigarettes, such as Liggett's *Piedmont* and American's *Sweet Caporals* began their slow decline. This pack is shown on page 27.

By Reynolds' death in July, 1918, his firm had accumulated 40% of American cigarette production. The stage was set for the great brand rivalries of the 1920s and 1930s. The first memorable slogan generated by Reynolds' Tobacco was 'I'd walk a mile for a Camel', which appeared throughout America in 1921. 'Let your own taste be the judge. Try Camels for yourself. A few smooth, refreshing puffs and you'd walk a mile for a Camel too', ran the copy. The slogan appears to have been aban-doned in the 1930s, but, interestingly, it was revived in the early Seventies, perhaps one of the earliest examples of tobacco nostalgia to be consciously used by the trade. One such advertise-ment from 1973 which ingeniously alludes to the old slogan shows the smoker having heard the call and abandoned his fishing basket oblivious to the chance of catching any fish. No understanding of the history and character of American advertising can be achieved without coming to terms with the great battles that took place between *Camel*, *Chesterfield*, and our next classic brand, *Lucky Strike*.

Lucky Strike

The American Tobacco Company under the leadership of Percival Hill and his dynamic son, George Washington Hill, came up with *Lucky Strike* as an answer to Reynolds' *Camel* in January, 1917. The brand name was originally used by RA Patterson of Richmond, Virginia, for a sliced plug tobacco. Duke acquired Patterson's firm in 1905 and the

'It's Toasted' implies the existence of a unique process, something not enjoyed by any other leaf. To emphasize the message early advertisements showed bread on a toasting fork. 'Doesn't a potato taste better when cooked?', ran the specious copy. Rivals scoffed at these implications, because the exposure to heat at some stage of the tobacco curing process was really quite common. But the public was persuaded. In a description of the Toasting Process published in his book, *The Story of Lucky Strike* (1938, New

into the cigarette-making machines. The whole atmosphere of the factory is that of the magic cave. Of the workers, Flanagan wrote, 'All of them seemed to be as relaxed as children engaged in a fascinating, familiar game.'

Lucky Strike's Visual Impact
George Washington Hill, fresh from his triumph in reviving the ailing *Pall Mall* cigarette, turned *Lucky Strike* into a successful brand. The story of the advertising campaign is told on pages 92–93. By 1930, *Lucky Strike* had

name was inherited by the American Tobacco Company on the dissolution of the Trust. *Lucky Strike* originally conjured up memories of the Gold Rush, of America's pioneer days, when a man could get rich and successful overnight. The original trademark showed a brawny arm, the hand brandishing a hammer. Patterson's had used the bull's eye motif for their plug and, with minor modifications, it was used for the *Luckies* pack in 1917. Camel used the slogan, 'I'd walk a mile . . .', *Chesterfield* the plain, 'They Satisfy', and *Luckies* the curious legend, 'It's Toasted'. The tobacco blend was very much the same as *Camel*, and perhaps for that reason the pack had to be easily distinguished, and the prime selling point had to be something special.

York's World Fair), Roy C Flanagan describes the leaves stripped of their stalks passing under a long battery of heaters. 'At intervals are dials watched by alert, young men who peer into the hot depths of the machines, turn cranks and, now and then, open little doors to look at the leaf that is passing through.' When he asked for more details of this toasting process he was told, 'It is, naturally, a closely guarded secret. It is the result of years spent in research to develop a light smoke.' The foreman turned a dial gently. 'Tobacco,' he added, 'is like a high strung thoroughbred colt . . .' The toasted tobacco goes on to be aired for twenty-four hours in a closed room, is shredded and then passes through into an ultra-violet ray machine. The alchemy is over, and after an eight day rest the raw material goes

achieved the impossible, it was outselling *Camel*. In 1933 *Chesterfield* also overtook *Camel*.

In the American campaigns the packs themselves were in constant attendance, usually dominating the foreground of the advertisement or poster, being offered by one eager smoker to another. The *Lucky Strike* was, to many people, the most visually effective of the 'Big Three'. *Camel* as a brand name was redolent of the East, *Chesterfield*, with aristocratic overtones, drifted the same way, while *Lucky Strike* was unmistakably American, with no foreign imagery, no visuals to distract.

The first *Lucky Strike* pack, based on Patterson's plug, showed a large red disc with gold surround, circled by a thick, black contour. The lettering is bold, without any loops or serifs in the central bull's eye that contains the brand name and the slogan, 'It's Toasted'. The brand name, with its associations of the Gold Rush, was also unmistakably American. Other tobacco brands used the theme – *49 cut plug*, for instance, showed miners panning for gold, *Pike's Peak* tobacco had on the label a bandit-like prospector resting from his labours on a hillside, hacking off a lump of tobacco to chew. The trademark on the side of the *Lucky* pack, the Indian chief, increases this traditional element.

constantly forced to look at the bull's eye. In *Alvo* (Azores) the arrow has hit the target. The Your Name *Selecto-matic* pack, an obvious trademark infringement, with its satirical version of the Lucky slogan, relied on the good humour of the company to escape. Others have not been so fortunate. It is one thing to be influenced by pack designs, it is another to exploit them, like the *Lucky Strike* toilet paper, and, in Thailand, the *Lucky Strike* condom that was marketed complete with the 'It's Toasted' slogan.

shelf.

The *Lucky Strike* packet also has the distinction of being almost the only pack to be used by a serious artist before the decade of Pop Art. Modern collage work has not shown a preference for the tobacco packet. Neither Picasso nor Braque seemed to have had an eye for the cigarette pack discarded in the café. Only the American painter Stuart Davis (1894–1964) seems to have been inspired by the modernity of pack art. In 1921 he painted *Lucky Strike* in New York, an elegant, almost heraldic

Other 'Lucky' Packs

The idea of 'Lucky' tobacco is one that crops up over and over again, both in pack design and in brand names. In a primitive way, the pack of cigarettes is a talisman against fate. It is an old French superstition that, in the face of the incomprehensible or threatening, the man with his hand in his pocket touches his left testicle for luck. Perhaps the pack is meant to provide alternative consolation. There are scores of 'Lucky' brandnames, *Lucky Dream*, (UK), *Lucky Boy* (Malta), *Lucky Choice* (UK), and *Lucky Find* (UK). Games of chance feature prominently, *Straight Flush* (UK), *Poker* (various countries) and *Treble Chance* (UK).

Gallaher's *Darts* (UK) is one of the many throughout the world that use the target as a central motif; the eye is

Lucky Strike's Design

The real *Lucky Strike* pack has the simplest elements, the only typographic extravagance allowed is the cinema-scope swell of the lettering to 'Cigarettes'. The red disc on a green ground achieves maximum colour contrast by exploiting the phenomenon known to designers and artists for centuries, complementary colours. 'A red design on a green ground shows up more distinctly, and is much more harmonious than a red on a blue or a red on violet,' writes GH Hurst in his *Handbook of the Theory of Colour* (London, 1900).

Hence with the maximum colour contrast, the simple elements, *Lucky Strike* as it looked before the pack change of 1942, was probably the most immediately visible brand on the tobacconist's

re-assemblage of the elements of the famous design, the bull's eye, the revenue stamp, trademark and lettering slotted into each other. Davis also painted *Cigarette Papers*, a Cubist celebration of the *Rizla* packet, and *Sweet Caporal*, in an attempt 'to selectively juxtapose various aspects of a subject or several unrelated objects', as he put it. The artist's father was a sign writer specializing in lettering, so he had a special awareness and sympathy for the world of commercial packaging.

The *Lucky Strike* pack in red and green lasted until 1942 when, according to the company, war austerities caused a change to a basic white ground. The true reason, according to one source, had more to do with pack design than patriotism.

Chesterfield and Marlboro

Two of America's best known cigarettes are grouped here together, Liggett & Myers' *Chesterfield* and Philip Morris' *Marlboro*, the first, a major contender for brand supremacy in the 1930s with a pack design that has hardly changed over the years, the other, one of America's most successful contemporary brands that has altered its pack design in a way very unusual in the tobacco industry.

Chesterfield was launched by Liggett & Myers in 1912, a year before Reynolds' *Camel*. In the 1920s the brand was repackaged to compete with *Lucky Strike* and *Camel*, changing its old-fashioned hull-and-slide, and following them into the soft pack of paper and foil. During the 1920s these three brands accounted for nearly 95% of the American cigarette market. The *Chesterfield* soft pack design combines heraldic devices, a sort of padded armchair back over a wasp-waist, and calligraphic flourishes printed over a distant prospect of a Turkish harbour, presumably one exporting tobacco. This motif serves to underline a particularly important theme – that the blend used for the cigarette was of Turkish and American tobaccos.

The hull-and-slide shown here is not from the 1920s, it is a complimentary pack of about 1950, close to the original design. Comparing it with a recent pack it is obvious how little has been allowed to change. The small alterations are however interesting in revealing more about that business beloved of the pack artist, 'tidying up'. Look at the lettering; the hull is still embellished with the decorative features shown in the Twenties, the 'f' in *Chesterfield* still has the barb and the blob that swells before the flourish comes to an end. The great billow of the 'S' at the end of 'cigarettes' is the last echo of the exuberance of letter forms that we have seen in other early packs.

The general design is basically a non-assertive exercise in typography set against the oddly top-heavy heraldic devices. Perhaps, in its clean lines, overall whiteness and thin horizontal banding, the pack seeks to promote the idea of mildness that is featured so widely throughout the advertising devoted to the product, 'it is Chesterfield's mildness – its entire freedom from harshness or irritation – that appeals so unfailingly to critical Smokers' (1931), 'The best cigarette

for you to smoke – Milder, *much* Milder' (1949). On the back of the *Chesterfield* pack from the mid-1950s there is an uncharacteristically defensive bit of copy, 'For a full year now, a medical specialist has given a group of Chesterfield smokers thorough examinations every two months. He reports no adverse effects to their nose, throat or sinuses from smoking Chesterfields.' With this emphasis on mildness, the slogan associated with the firm, 'They Satisfy', takes on a new significance. Mild they may be, but 'they sure hit the smoking spot'.

Like all successful cigarette packs, *Chesterfield* has attracted its fair share of imitators, and one of them has survived in the Ventegodt collection. How many smokers in Peru have picked up a pack of *Country Club* thinking they were *Chesterfield*. There have been some ingenious changes. The Turkish harbour has now become a building, the leather chair back so familiar from the American pack has been turned into an even stranger bricked-up construction surmounted by a radiant sun motif. Yet the Peruvian pack clearly conserves that rather aristocratic imagery of the *Chesterfield* pack, largely because of the elegant plagiarism of the lettering.

Tobacco companies jealously guard their visual identities, and particularly the trade names they have adopted. Although it is not known if *Country Club* came to the attention of Liggett & Myers, most companies are prepared to spend hundreds of thousands of dollars or pounds to defend their identities, because confusions, either deliberately created, or brought about accidentally, can be even more expensive. Incidentally, cigarette firms insist on exactly the right shade of colour on their packs. Less intense reds permitted by the printer could easily lead to mistakes by the consumer, and loss of sales.

If *Chesterfield* has hardly changed its pack design over the years, then that other classic brand *Marlboro* has gone through a totally unprecedented process – the Sex Change operation. It is a brand long associated with manly vigour, and a devil-may-care attitude to life. In the 1950s tennis coaches and weather-beaten athletes growled at us through clenched teeth that Marlboro 'sure delivers the goods'. In recent years the product has been particularly associated with the basic challenges faced by the pioneer – the cowboy battling on the open range against the pressure of natural forces – 'Come to where the flavor is. Come to Marlboro

Country.' The pack reinforces this image with its sharp angularity of red chevron on the front and back, repeated along the bottom of the pack for easier identification when stacked in a tobacconist's shop. The lettering also has a no-frills vertical thrust, particularly to the 'l' and 'b' which tend to add to the illusion that the pack is bigger than it is.

Marlboro Country originally was shown as a reality, a simple photograph – the cowboy with white hat and lassoo, cigarette clamped firmly in his mouth. 'The great strength of the Marlboro Country campaign,' said Jack Landry of Philip Morris USA, to the San Francisco Chronicle (November 1971), 'is in the last couple of years, with so much controversy, and so much about our life today that is frustrating to people, with people up to their ears, that we never beat anybody over the head. We are reflecting a period that had none of that controversy in it, the days of the pioneer, the cowboy. The bad guys wore black hats, the good guys wore white ones. Everything was simple and uncomplicated or at least that's the attitude of the average person in this country.'

Astonishingly, *Marlboro* was launched in America in 1925 by Philip Morris & Company, (a cigarette of the same name had been marketed by the original British firm), chiefly as a lady's cigarette. The denizens of Marlboro Country would surely have curled their lips at the *Marlboro Beauty Tips*, a pack containing cigarettes with tips coloured red to conceal those tell-tale lipstick traces. To prevent embarrassing mistakes, this variety was printed with an illusionist tear as if revealing the massed ranks of red tips.

The brand was introduced in this way, 'Husbands told their wives what a rare new treat they could serve for their friends and week-end guests.' In November, 1926, readers of *Vanity Fair* were informed that in one short year Marlboro cigarettes 'have found a place of honour in pockets and hand-bags in almost every club and community in the United States . . . They lend an added charm to smoking. Mild as May, 20 for 20 cents'. The regular pack, shown on page 42, reiterated this elite image of smoking, classically balanced, with that exclusive air that only the ratifying signature can bring. The post-war pack, while clinging to the last remains of the Morris coat-of-arms, removes all traces of this decadence, replaces charm with challenge, relaxation with alertness, the specific with the general.

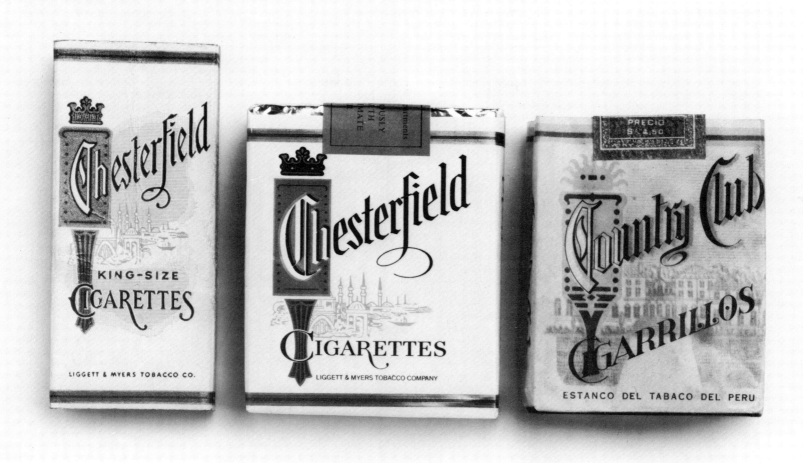

Habanera of Bolivia

If cigarette pack art in Europe and North America tended to become simpler and more immediate in its impact on the eye, South American packs retained, until quite recently, an exuberance of decoration that is quite unique. Features familiar to European packs are multiplied and elaborated to extraordinary lengths, an elegant curl of ribbon becomes a frenetic, tangled skein, a sober grouping of medals awarded to the product is converted by the South American designer into a treasure chest of coins, cups, medals, stars and sashes awarded at obscure exhibitions in minor provincial capitals. Whereas the European designer has at least pondered the problem of making the brand name stand out, his counterpart in Bolivia throws practical considerations to the winds, seeking first

to amuse, entertain and bewilder.

These delightful features are best represented by *Habanera*, a Bolivian brand, available in three packs which, while keeping their family resemblance, create distinctive identities. No area of the pack is allowed to remain undecorated. Even the sections of paper destined to disappear in the gluing share in the designer's scheme. The three packs share a love of flowers, tendril, blossom and leaf, printed in brilliant colours. These forms merge imperceptibly with swollen plaques and stylized frames, in which the trained eye can search for entwined initials and trademarks. *Habanera's* range of medals is, however, positively modest compared with one Cuban pack showing twenty-six individual medals.

A delightful feature of the South American Baroque style is the dominating figure of the Goddess of the Pack, symbolic of some deeper purpose than the mere titillation of the smoker's palette. Like similar packs from

Ecuador, Peru and Paraguay, *Habanera* employs the Goddess to embody in earnest gesture and suitable attribute, stern and worthy national characteristics. Here *Habanera No 1* presides solemnly over emblems of Bolivia. The Goddess of *Habanera No 2* rests, seemingly exhausted, among emblems of industry, while *No 3* embodies the spirit of national law. All three packs reproduced are for soft cup 20s and qualify for the designation 'Classic Pack' for their robust gaiety and inventive use of available surfaces.

Many packs feature sexy ladies, chiefly of the smouldering, flashing eyed beauty type. In the Ventegodt collection there is a brand called *Muy Amor*. A sultry society beauty lifts her cigarette to a lighter in the palm of her hand that, on closer examination, turns out to be a human heart, aflame with passion.

With the internationalization of the cigarette industry, this bravado and colour has been largely inhibited.

CHAPTER FOUR

SAILORS AND THE SEA

Images of the Sea, of Sailors and Ships occur constantly on the pack fronts of the world. Sometimes they reflect the old tobacco trade between America and Europe. Sometimes they celebrate the hardy open-air life of the 20th-century mariner. This chapter is presided over by the most famous Cigarette Sailor, John Player's Hero trademark, first registered in 1891.

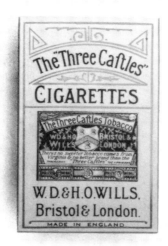

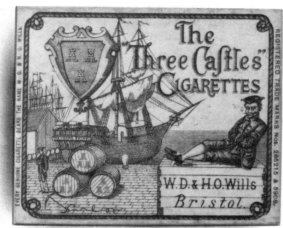

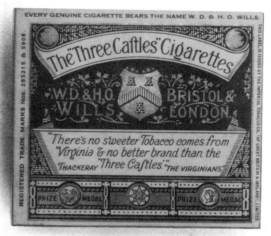

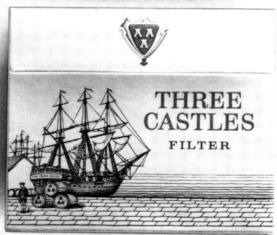

Three Castles and the Early Tobacco Trade

Although it was a design that exploited the contemporary preoccupation with the sea, the *Three Castles* pack brought back memories of the seventeenth-century tobacco trade and particularly the port of Bristol. The brand was introduced in 1877 by Wills as a pipe tobacco, and a year later as a high grade cigarette, hand-made and probably sold by weight. By 1884 the brand was being made on a machine along with other Wills' brands, *Gold Flake* and *Louisville*. In 1890 they were sold in 'a sliding case', the sort of hull-and-slide shown upper left. The subsequent development of the pack design is a classic case of modernization, where a wealth of imagery is abandoned for a simpler, more visible pack. Modifications appeared as a result of changes in pack technology (see Introduction).

The original hull-and-slide pack front with green, blue and gold design remained virtually unchanged from about 1900 until the introduction of the hinged lid carton in 1956. The brand name was originally coined by George Waterston, an Edinburgh tradesman who suggested to Wills that a Bristol firm should use the name Thackeray invented for a brand of tobacco in *The Virginians*.

The pack front is one of the more memorable in the industry, and based on 'a picturesque old engraving' (as yet untraced), but it also has an affinity with eighteenth-century tobacco labels. The back shows a classic mustering of label, ribbon, floral ornament, motto, trademark and medal (a 20 pack). The original *Three Castles* pack of 20 cigarettes showed two figures on the front, one a solitary sailor, standing on the quay, the other a man sitting on a packing case, probably the black slave symbolic in the public's mind with the Virginia tobacco plantations. The harbour is obviously Bristol, one of the major ports for the Tobacco Trade for many years.

Since the design was copied from an engraving, and then copied again, it is not surprizing that certain nautical inaccuracies were further compounded. The disposition of the shrouds, the yards and sails, are inaccurate, as is the curious garden hut that appears on the deck of the ship, *The Young Rachel*. In 1956 the first hinged lid pack was introduced, and the lettering was moulded into greater visibility, and the rope frame suitably adapted. The revised design of July, 1966 (not shown) dispensed with the rope frame, and, to stop the slave falling off the packing case, a stout wooden post was sunk in the cobbles. From 1968 his familiar face had gone, replaced by the brand name that at least now remained visible when the top was flipped. A similar concept to *Three Castles* was used by Carreras for their *Virginia* cigarettes (1937).

The *Three Castles* may have been inspired by Thackeray's text but it does use an idea found world-wide, the appeal of the number 'Three'. Here is just a small proportion of the vast range of 'Three' packs: *Three General* (Seng Lee Tobacco Co, Singapore), *Three Birds* (UK, Gallaher's), *Three Dogs* (UK, anon), *Three Roses* (UK, Wills), *Three Nuns* (UK, Bells), *Three Pagodas* (Thailand), *Three Kings* (USA, Union Tobacco Co) and *Three Sisters* (Singapore, East Asia Tobacco Co). Three, as a number, has many symbolic meanings, but in this context probably helps to convince the smoker that his pack will bring him luck.

Three Castles represented the Tobacco Industry's vision of itself in an age of mass production. One of the most famous trademarks, Player's Hero, (the sailor in the lifebelt reproduced on page 62 and described on page 64), from the Player's *Medium Navy Cut* pack, represents very much the same idea, but in a military context more suitable to the early 1900s.

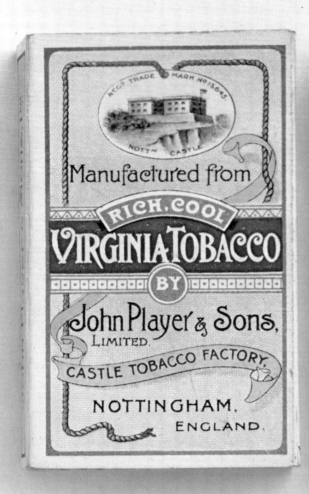

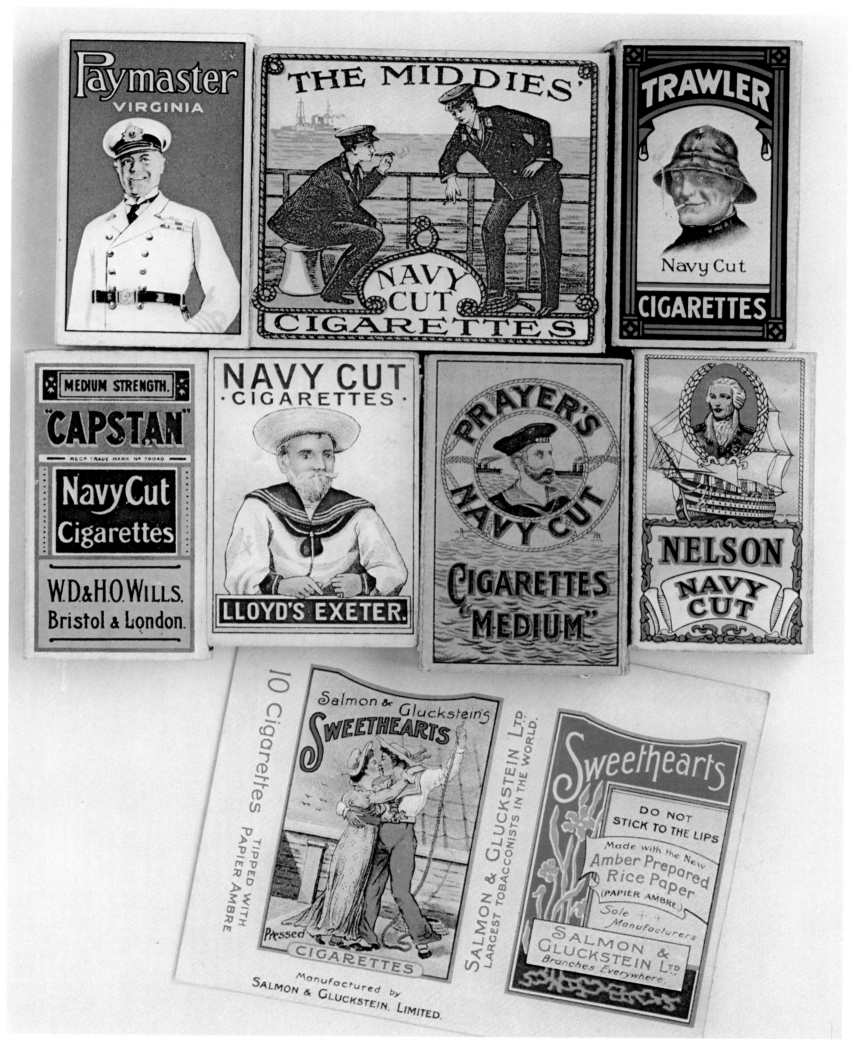

Naval and Nautical

Player's Navy Cut

The term 'Navy Cut' is so common that its roots are often forgotten. During the nineteenth century, and our own, sailors in the Royal Navy were allowed to buy whole tobacco leaves which they compressed into rolls of tobacco with tight windings of rope. Shredded tobacco, usually for smoking in a pipe, could be got by slicing the end of the roll thinly.

Player's famous and evocative *Hero* first *HMS Dreadnought*, built in 1875. The design expressed pride in Britain's nautical power during a period when there was public anxiety at the growth of the German Navy. It also tuned in with the Tobacco Industry's own vision of itself, the old established firm marketing the products of the twentieth century. The image of the sailor combines the manly vigour of the sentinel with the healthy glow of the Old Salt.

Player's *Navy Cut* cigarettes were launched in 1900 at 3d for 10. By 1907 the brand was, next to Wills' *Woodbine*, Britain's largest selling cigarette. The *Navy Cut* pack was so successful that it some of the British sailor packs that show a family resemblance to *Hero*. Two brands are worth closer study. Lauralf's *The Middies* (UK, about 1910) and Salmon & Gluckstein's *Sweethearts* (UK, 1905). *The Middies* uses the motif of two midshipmen relaxing on board ship, surrounded by a rope frame reminiscent of the *Three Castles* pack. The *Sweethearts* wrapping shown is a paper 10. The design is a rare, light-hearted nautical pack, showing a sailor saying goodbye to his sweetheart. The copy on the back of the wrapper assures the lovers that 'Sweethearts do *not* stick to the lips . . . Made with Amber

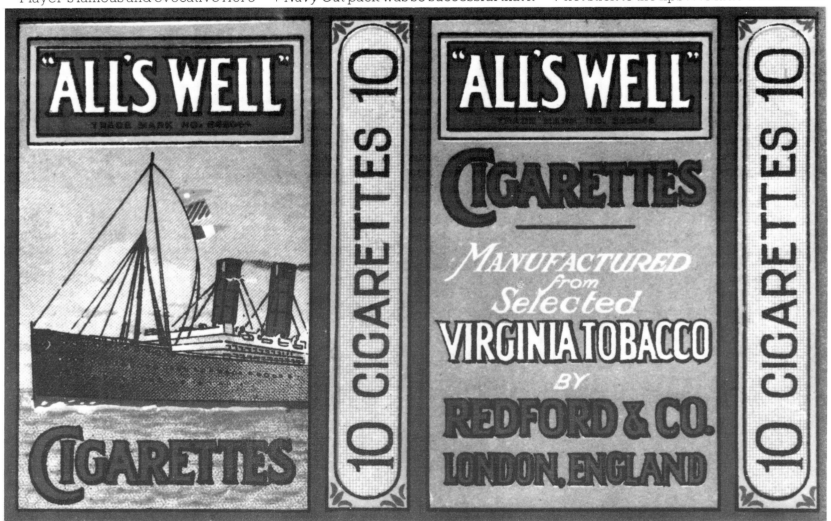

trademark, shown on page 62, was assembled over a period of years. The sailor's head was registered in 1883 for Player's *Navy Cut* pipe tobacco. He was put inside the lifebelt and lettered in 1888. Three years later, he was registered in his present form. The sailor, so the legend goes, was Thomas Huntley Wood, who served in the 1880s on *HMS Edinburgh*. In exchange for the use of his face, he was given a pouchful of tobacco and a handful of guineas.

To Hero's left is a three-decker, reputed to be *HMS Britannia*, one of the biggest ships of the line of her day. Significantly, the sailor turns purposively to the more modern counterpart, the

attracted many imitators. Note the pack produced by Tokei & Company, of Japan, under the unlikely trade name, John Prayer's, Paradise Factory, London, England. This obvious infringement was duly noticed and suppressed by BAT.

The design of Player's *Navy Cut* remained basically the same until March, 1942, when monochrome paper wrappers were introduced as a wartime economy (see page 102). Board was only made available for cigarette packs again in 1950.

Other Sailor Packs

On the previous page are included Prepared Rice Paper'. The back of the wrapper incorporates a very attractive stylized iris pattern. Cunningly, the designer has shown the plant's roots in the panel beneath the maker's name.

On these pages is a group of British packs showing the national fascination with ships and the sea, the surface and textures of water, the dynamic shapes that cleave through the waves. Particularly powerful are Redford's *All's Well* cigarettes, and Salmon & Gluckstein's *Life Boat Navy Cut*. Included on page 65 is the more domestic Chinese pack, *Homeward Junk* (about 1930), and the reassuring Mexican pack *Faros*, which is, incidentally, still on sale.

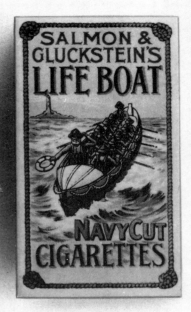

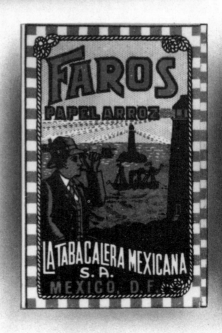

Life on the Ocean Wave

Rather than dwell too much on the social side of life on the ocean wave, the long round of deck quoits, cocktails and the Captain's table, many brands appealed more to people's aspirations to lead the life of the rich globe-trotter, or trans-Atlantic traveller. The pack artist loved above all the dramatic silhouette of the ship breasting the waves, seen here on the *Asahi* pack (Japan), *Manhattan* (Swiss export), *Faros* (Mexico), *Twin Screw* (UK) and *America* (Argentina). It is interesting that two of the designs, *Asahi* and *America*, show the vessel leaving port, set against the dynamic skyline of the Skyscraper City. The *America* pack even makes the same point as the Player's *Navy Cut*, modernity and tradition, luxury liner and galleon.

Packs using the imagery of the sea make up probably the largest thematic group, military and civilian, benevolent and aggressive. Given the average layman's knowledge of nautical matters, given the average graphic designer's awareness of the intricacies of rigging and the like, it is hardly surprising that mistakes were made in depictions on packs. The inaccuracies in the *Three Castles* design are perhaps excusable; according to Geoffrey Bennett, the editor at Mardon, Son & Hall, the eighteenth-century Bristol privateer seldom had the main sail slung between the mast and shrouds. 'Another is the missing set of shrouds on the port side, and a complete absence of yards and sails on the mizen mast.' The modern pack does at least try to get the details right, as well as adding a missing row of gun ports.

If this seems a trifle perfectionist, the case of Player's *Navy Cut* Hero is perhaps less excusable. In 1883 the sailor appeared with one stripe only on his collar. At some time before the amalgamation with the Imperial Tobacco Company, another stripe was added to his collar. In this shape the design was registered as a trademark. Discovering that, in fact, the sailor should have three stripes, Player's ultimately decided that the mistake would have to stay unchanged, and so it survives to the present day. There was another error that caused mild embarrassment when it was pointed out to Player's, that the cap ribbon read merely HERO. In the original design the artist forgot the HMS, and, again, once registered, the mistake had to stay.

If *Three Castles* and Player's *Navy Cut* were trapped into minor errors, then the case of Wills' *Pirate* surely constitutes a design howler. The brand was launched in 1887, together with *Diamond Queen* (page 70), as a two-pronged export drive in the South African market. The two brands must have presented a combination of Empire mindedness and swaggering recklessness. Messrs Holt of Kimberley were appointed by Wills as agents for selling them.

The cigarette did well throughout the world, and the moustachioed buccaneer, standing against a typical 'Hero'-type seascape and sky, and armed to the teeth, became a well known brand character. On the back of the pack it is revealed that he is fresh from bloody battles at sea. The brand was also sold on the home market. The basic format of the design had to be flexible, capable of being expanded to a tin label. Tins were preferred as containers for cigarettes when the climate was extremely variable. Originally the cannon behind the Pirate was fixed to the deck with a short piece of rope attached to a giant sized cleat. When the design came to be rationalized, date unknown, it was felt that 'the big wing-nut' looked silly, so it was replaced by a simple length of rope passing through the ring on the cannon. Almost immediately it was pointed out that the lay of the rope (the way it is twisted) changes mysteriously as it passes through the ring.

CHAPTER FIVE

PEOPLE ON PACKS

All sorts of people have appeared on the front of the cigarette pack to help sell the product. For some cigarettes a brand character was created, the Kensitas Butler, Herbert Tareyton, or the Philip Morris bell-boy Johnnie. Even cultural heroes were enlisted, such as Dante, Shelley, Chaplin and Tarzan. Cigarette smoking, they all maintained, was a great luxury.

Brand Characters

Finding a character, often in cartoon form, to represent a product in the public's mind, is a favourite device of the advertiser, to personalize what is, very often, a boring or mundane article. The power of brand characters cannot be overestimated, they attract children, always the consumer's most vulnerable spot, and they mobilize sympathy. The British firm Tate & Lyle created Mr Cube to help them in their successful campaign to prevent nationalization of the sugar industry.

Before 1960 many cigarettes were presented to the consumer by jaunty minor aristocrats, usually British, terribly sporty, beaming and ever so slightly stupid. The flashy Sir Park Drive (UK, Gallaher) appears on a *Park Drive* slide, popping up as you take a cigarette. *Patrick* (Germany) shows another variant on the John Bull figure, a shade Pickwickian, although boasting 'Good Tobaccos from USA'.

Tetley's *Oracle* (UK) and *Passing Show* (UK, Gallaher) create a very similar sort of figure, jovial and top-hatted. *Sir William* (Holland, General Tobacco Co, about 1930) venerable in appearance, watchful under his jaunty cap, provides a more sober image.

It was to inject English sophistication into an American cigarette that the Falk Tobacco Company of 45th Street, New York, created the Tareyton Toff to accompany their *Herbert Tareyton London Cigarettes*, launched in 1913 at 'Twenty for a Quarter'. With his top hat, high collar, swagger stick and obligatory monocle, he beams out from behind the brand slogan, 'There's *something* about them you'll like', a rather plaintive, ambiguous line. In the 1920s on packs, pack inserts, posters and advertisements, he is to be found at the forefront of all classy gatherings, at the race track, tennis court and cocktail bar, hand casually in pocket of immaculate pin-stripe trousers, asking 'Have you tried that Extraordinary Cigarette . . .?' In the 1950s, and a property of the American Tobacco Company, he was maintaining his contacts with the élite; he appeared alongside America's leading hostesses.

In the 1960s Tareyton's Toff was pensioned off, and the brand image drastically restructured. The brand name shrank to mere *Tareyton*, the crown was discretely simplified, and the elegant Herbert replaced by the more democratic image of a young man,

identity unspecified, clean shaven. He is no longer shown in art work, but in a photograph. He is bare headed and in a casual polo neck sweater. Most significantly of all, the monocle has been replaced by a black eye, explained by the slogan, 'Us Tareyton smokers would rather fight than switch.' The symbol of aristocracy has been neatly changed into a symbol of aggression.

One alternative to the creation of the fictitious cartoon character is the use of the big name to sell the product, such as John Lund's testimonial for *Chesterfield* (page 104) or the appearance of the 'Kings of Sport' series for the same brand (tennis player Bobby Rigg, golf's Lloyd Mangrum).

Another alternative is to link the

product with dead cultural and political heroes. To give the cigarette that extra edge of class all manner of dignified figures were enlisted by the advertiser, Sir Walter Scott on the British brand *Waverley*, *Shelley* (UK), *Tolstoi* (USA), *Teddy* (Norway, a salute to Teddy Roosevelt) and most unlikely of all, *Dante* (country unidentified). In art, *Rembrandt*, the *Discobolus* and *Mona Lisa* have all been signed up.

Certain associations are now unacceptable, Tarzan's manly form (Malaysia) yields place to Brown & Williamson's *Tramps*, on sale first in 1974, where under the slogan, 'The gentle smoke', Chaplin strikes characteristic poses, affably foolish, comically seedy and very urban.

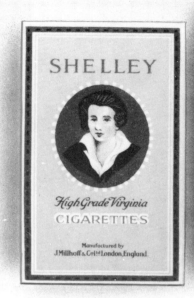

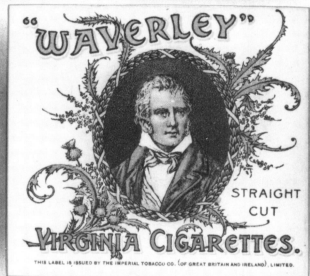

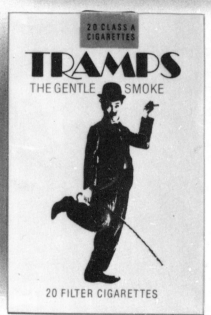

The Upper Crust

In 1893 Wills tried to register a cigarette brand called *Royal George*, presumably dedicated to the future George V. Permission was refused, and the brand was subsequently re-named *Capstan*, one of the most successful British brands of the twentieth century. Apart from the much-prized Royal coat-of-arms, and the 'By Appointment' sign that shows their patronage, the British Royal Family do not allow direct references to themselves on packages for any product.

Cigarette companies all over the world have constantly linked their product with national characteristics and virtues, a concept that had become increasingly difficult with the growing internationalization of the industry. It was much easier to create a patriotic, even chauvinistic design in the first decade of this century, for example with BMG's *British Standard* (UK, about 1907), 'The Sun never sets on this Flag'

The hierarchy of aristocracy and monarchy is used in Lambert & Butler's *Belted Earl* (UK, about 1905) set at a medieval tournament, and Hignett's *Crown Jewels* (UK, 1915) with its stately frame of national emblems.

Many of these brands were exported and carried the image of Great Britain

to all parts of the world. How resolute Britannia looks on Player's *Island Queen* pack (UK, 1902), set in her frame of English roses. Presumably foreign smokers would have puzzled over the fact that the great metropolitan centres, London, Cardiff, Liverpool and Glasgow are thought not sufficiently important for indication on the map, while Nottingham, the seat of John Player's Tobacco Factory, reigns supreme.

But images of the British Royal Family did, in fact, appear on packs. In 1897, Queen Victoria consented to appear on Wills' new *Diamond Queen*, part of the export drive to South Africa. Even when the Diamond Jubilee was over, the

word still had particular significance for South Africa, because of its diamond mining. The pack, our example of which is dated April 1910, containing 10 cigarettes with mouthpieces, is a distinguished combination of printing and embossing. Later the popularity of Edward, Prince of Wales (to become, briefly, Edward VIII), and his reputation for informality, led to his appearance on the *Prince Charming* pack (UK, about 1930). Little is known of this brand, but again, it may have been for export. *Windsor*, too, was for export, showing the Prince's face presiding over the wooded slopes and Castle at Windsor, one of the homes of the Royal Family that is featured constantly on packs, on *Windsor Castle* exported to America,

and on *Windsor Turkish* cigarettes. Other Royal haunts featured are *Palace* cigarettes and *Park Royal*.

Surprizingly in view of America's republican traditions there are examples of companies using royalist imagery, Reynolds' *Prince Albert* (a smoking tobacco, marketed from 1907) and Benson & Hedges' *His Majesty's Cigarette* (1910). More typically, *Pall Mall* was dedicated to 'His Imperial Majesty the American Gentleman'. However, to add dignity and Old World sophistication to the more expensive cigarettes, a host of princelings and minor nobilities were paid lavish retainers to look haughty on advertisements, juxtaposed with their florid

signatures and credentials.

The modern association between smoking and Royalty has to be more subtle. Claims have been made that the designers of the *Rothman's King Size* pack based their design on a picture of the Duke of Edinburgh in naval uniform. If the hinged lid is partly open, so the story goes, the filter tips present the equivalent of the tanned face, the lid design approximates the cap and the round blue design further down can be interpreted as a naval jacket.

The appeals to the aristocratic life had less exalted levels however. If you could only gaze in awe at the Royal presence, then in the image of the Toff and his servant you had, at least, something to which to aspire.

Upstairs and Downstairs

Before the rise of the Universal cigarette (see pages 124–125) the product was particularly associated with class distinctions. In the wonderful world of the pack there reclines, Upstairs, a Bertie Wooster figure, projected through an aggressively sported monocle (such as *Hallo*, UK). This breed of Toff spread widely, to Norway for *Gentleman*, to the United States for *Herbert Tareyton*, and in a distorted form to Denmark's *Bobby*.

Downstairs we discover the servile figure of the butler, or perhaps a bell-hop, bearing on a silver tray the prized pack of cigarettes, and with a glow of anticipation at his master's delight in being handed exactly the right brand. The most celebrated Jeeves-type figure on the packs is the *Kensitas* butler, here appearing on the *K4's* pack, 'Your cigarettes, Sir . . . and four for your friends'. Despite the authentic combination of dignity and professionalism, the butler was, in fact, a male model who had been signed up by Wix & Sons after he made an appearance at the British and Empire Exhibition in 1926. His best known American counterpart was 'Johnnie', cheekier and more extrovert. His distinctive appearance, he was 48 inches tall, and his cry of 'Calling Philip Morris', made him on advertisements, radio commercials and indeed on the packs themselves, 'the world's most famous living trademark,' as the company put it.

According to an article in the *San Francisco Chronicle* (October 16, 1974) on the retirement of the 'MFLTM', John Louis Roventini had been working at the New Yorker Hotel, featured as 'the smallest bell-boy in the world', when, as the story goes, the then Vice-President of Sales for Philip Morris, and Milton Blow, president of Morris' advertising agency, asked him to page 'Philip Morris'. So impressed were they with his clarion call that he was signed up on the spot at $100 a week to advertise the firm's products. An instant hit, Johnnie was appearing in as many as four live radio shows a day from 1933 to 1947, and then, dressed in his famous red and black uniform, starring in the new TV ads.

Johnnie was, however, only one of the many perky bell-hops seen around the tobacco trade, usually advancing upon the consumer with a winsome grin and a silver tray of cigarettes. Such is Wix' *Page Boy* (UK, with, on the back, the

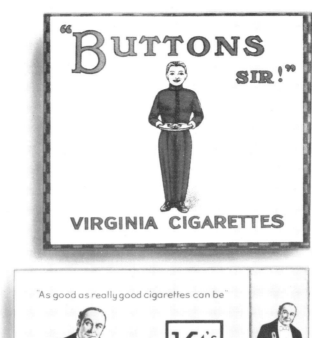

famous slogan, 'It's a Pleasure, Sir!' written over a large seal of quality). Ronne's *Buttons Sir!* (UK, Ronne's) shows how limited was this field of imagery. The design of Arrow's *Bell-boy* (UK) varies the effect in a very subtle way. The illustration on the back of the pack shows the bell-boy some distance away, down the sun deck of the luxury liner. On the front he is now within reach of the sun-soaked traveller.

Upstairs we find the ultimate destination of the butler and bell-boy, the Young Master. In *Hallo* (UK, about 1925) he is in evening dress, peering in a rather brainless way at us through his monocle, as he guffaws on the phone. Barnett's *Statesman* (UK), Ogden's *Gentleman* (UK and a label for a 50 tin) and Marcovitch's *Black and White* (UK) show him in different moods, different

poses. And wherever countries needed to create that raffish but elegant aristocrat to sell cigarettes on the luxury levels, they called in the Toff, in Norway's *Gentleman*, Germany's *Kreller*, and in the Danish version of the Bull Dog Breed, *Bobby*.

If the Toff has largely been forced out of business (see page 68 for the change in image of the Tareyton Toff), his modern counterpart, suave, poised and distinguished, takes the more potentially aggressive form of *Max* (St James Tobacco Co), exuding all the savoir-faire of James Bond. Morland & Company of Grosvenor Street, London, and Ian Fleming's tobacconists, actually sold a brand called *James Bond No 1* and *No 2*, accompanied by the brand name *Three Rings*, Bond's cigarettes in Ian Fleming's spy thrillers.

The Easy Life

Smoking must be seen as pleasurable, but of course not too pleasurable – not a word about addiction unless it was in the context of the lure of the seductive East. With the prevailing aristocratic image of smoking in the 1920s and 1930s, it is no surprise to find great emphasis on smoking as an enhancement of the joys of lazy living, whether it be after a tennis match in Martin's *Ranelagh* (UK, about 1935, where even the lettering has had time to cultivate extra curlicues), or while being driven by one's chauffeur, as in *Motor Cigarettes* (UK, about 1935).

Two brands make particularly interesting points about the promotion of tobacco products. Teofani's *West End* cigarettes show the Toff and Butler together in an acceptable context, London's Clubland. The creation of clubland associations was a common device for selling a product. Other packs stress it, such as *Army Club*.

Probably the most characteristic of packs displaying the elements of the Easy Life was Muratti's *After Lunch* cigarettes, here shown in two designs, the first of about 1910, and the second dating from the mid-1920s. In themselves they neatly illustrate the early impulses to tidy up pack imagery, the pruning away of plaques, cartouches, and *trompe l'oeil* ribbons.

The typography of the early pack lurches and leaps in asymetrical excesses. By the mid 1920s the brand and maker's names are strategically disposed for legibility, instead of fighting with a multi-coloured chequered floor. The 1920s scene is noticeably more healthy, set in an open verandah instead of the sultry, moist atmosphere of the hot-house with jungle palms. Most importantly, and perhaps because of a change in public advertising standards, the post-prandial cigarette accompanies a tray of coffee rather than the nip of something tawny and alcoholic in the bottle on the pre-war table. The whole concept of the *After Lunch* cigarette would be impossible today. What advertising agency would concede that half the day must elapse before the consumer is allowed to consume?

Yet if this appears too materialist, mere sensual gratification, it can be seen from the opening of the next chapter that there were no limitations to the fevered imaginings once the Smoker slept. Tobacco smoking always had to differentiate itself from opium smoking, but there were times when dreams, seduction and the sweet hint of oriental vices could sell the smoker these Lucky Dreams.

CHAPTER SIX

LUCKY DREAMS

Dreams, reveries and sweet seductions were all used to lure the would-be purchaser. If the scantily clad pin-up and *femme-fatale* on the pack were insufficient, then the smoker was offered access to the exotic mysteries of the Middle East, harems, pyramids and palm trees. Many designers relished the opportunity to introduce richness and colour, often with bizarre results.

Seduction East and West

The *Lucky Dream* cigarette, made by the Lucky Dream Cigarette Company, (a subsidiary of Osborne's of Portsmouth), is in itself a later version of a brand called *Miranda's Dream*. The change of brand character, from female to male, may have signified a change from a lady's to a gentleman's cigarette. The designer of *Lucky Dream* appears to have been inspired by that subject so beloved of the Old Masters, the seduction of Danae by Zeus (the Greek legend runs that he had to assume the form of a shower of gold in order to trick her into submission). The atmosphere of sex and temptation, created by the torrent of flowers and cigarettes that fall into the sleeper's lap in the palm lined conservatory, is further underlined by the Cupid whispering dangerous things into his sleeping ear.

Part of the smoker's dream was the seductive and beautiful woman, the pin-up of the pack such as *Gona* (UK, about 1905). She usually appears in two guises, the *femme fatale* and the slave of the harem. Murray's *Island Queen* (UK, about 1935) displays a syren of the rocks luring mariners to their doom in her close-fitting one-piece red costume and matching bathing cap, (or is it a hand-bag?). The 1930s Chinese pack, *Crab Beauty*, uses a nautical blend of pleasure and pain. The presence of Eve is never far from the cigarette pack – providing the seductive scenario *par excellence*. She is represented obliquely here in Salmon & Gluckstein's *Snake Charmer*, in which she also doubles as Cleopatra. America offers *Jezebel* and *Sin* cigarettes from the 1920s (not illustrated). Many of these brands were in fact perfumed cigarettes for the female market, scented with assorted shades of Gardenia, Amber Perfume and Rose. Denmark had a brand called *Blue Boy* Taste Cigarettes that had a sophisticated device built into the tip, a capsule of perfume that was broken with the fingers before the cigarette was smoked.

The dream of the white slave in the harem is widely used, particularly to emphasize the Turkish or Egyptian type of cigarette. She features in the *Harem* pack (UK, about 1935) and at her proudest in Major Drapkin's *Crayol* (UK, about 1900). It is interesting to note that in the last two packs the lettering responds to the exotic scene. In the *Harem* pack the designer has injected

considerable interest in the horizontal bars of the letters – note the 'E', pliant and shaped, almost wearing Turkish slippers with curly toes. Beneath the oval, studded frame, watch the 'A's' and 'H's' sag visibly in the middle.

The *Crayol* pack, a sleek handmaiden in a visibly Middle Eastern landscape, encourages an eccentric disregard of

spaced relationships, with its tumescent 'C', its stomping, extended serifs and the Egyptian hieroglyphic 'O'. The lettering on *Shamrock* has its own fascination too.

The popularity of Turkish and Egyptian cigarettes earlier in the century assured a maximum of Middle Eastern themes.

Egyptian Mysteries

Powerful and affluent societies very often look to the ancient civilizations as a ratification of their own cultural significance and economic energy. Although many tobacco merchants and entrepreneurs had established their businesses in Cairo and Alexandria, Egypt is not exactly associated with the cultivation of exotic tobacco leaf. Most of the exotic tobaccos are grown in the Balkans; Turkey and Greece are the major producers of high grade Oriental leaf. And yet packs empha-

whiff of the harem, the call of the desert. This probably underlies the American fascination for brand names beginning with *Egyptian* . . . Between 1900 and 1910 some of the brands you could buy were *Egyptian Prettiest*, *Heroes*, *Miracles*, *Palms*, and *Arabs*. Slightly more distinguished were the *Egyptiennes*, *Straights* and *Elegantes*.

Of the British brands, Morris' *Egyptian Blend* cigarettes offered a real roof-top idyll high over the streets of old Cairo, or at least what the artist thought old Cairo looked like. Under an ornamental hanging, a range of harem lovelies relax on rugs and silks. But it could be any other romantic venue for the armchair Eastern traveller.

boasted that their posters had even been stuck on the Pyramids themselves.

The *Prince of Egypt* cigarette box label (export to Denmark, about 1920) shows at least some signs of having looked at the original. While Teofani's *Pyramid* brand has a vision of the Pyramids communicated in a sort of shorthand, the American *Pyramid* box wrapper pares everything down to essentials. A group of three pyramids of primitive perspective appear in the desert, perhaps from beneath, constructed from vast stone blocks with bad mortar pointing. Two seedy palm trees of huge dimensions preside over the strange scene, the Sphinx having presumably fled.

sizing the Balkans are few, while Egyptian imagery has inspired many.

The fascination with the old Egyptian civilization is a constant feature of twentieth-century architecture and design, from the design of skyscrapers and cinemas to the Hollywood cinematic epics of the 1920s. No handbook of ornament was complete without a section devoted to Egyptian design. Archaeological discoveries during this period made people more aware of the Egyptian cultural achievement. On a less exalted plane, never far from people's minds was the image of the dangerous, passionate Middle East – the smouldering eyes of the insatiable Arab luring the innocent to his tent – the

When the pack designer wanted to evoke more positively the idea of Egypt, what better and more characteristic than the Pyramid of Cheops, the two subsidiary pyramids and the Giant Sphinx, five miles west of Giza. Apart from visual identity, the Pyramids had been studied intensively, measured and fitted to all manner of bizarre mystical systems. They were not only used by cigarette firms. In 1901 Pears used them to advertise their soap with the following adaptation of Longfellow, 'The mighty pyramids of stone/ That wedge-like cleave the desert airs,/When nearer seen and better known,/Are but gigantic steps of . . . Pears!' Some British advertisers

There were occasions when pack designers rose more lovingly and ingeniously to the challenge of Egyptian art. The most extravagant of this genre was the box label printed for *Mavrides Cigarettes*, produced by Alex S Mavrides at the Fashionable Cigarette Manufactory in Cairo. The label was probably produced by a British printer; it was not until recently that British-American Tobacco packaging like this was printed in the country of cigarette production. The design has all the hallmarks of the inspiration of Owen Jones' *Grammar of Ornament*. The elements are brilliantly and harmoniously combined and they look reasonably authentic. It is rarely so.

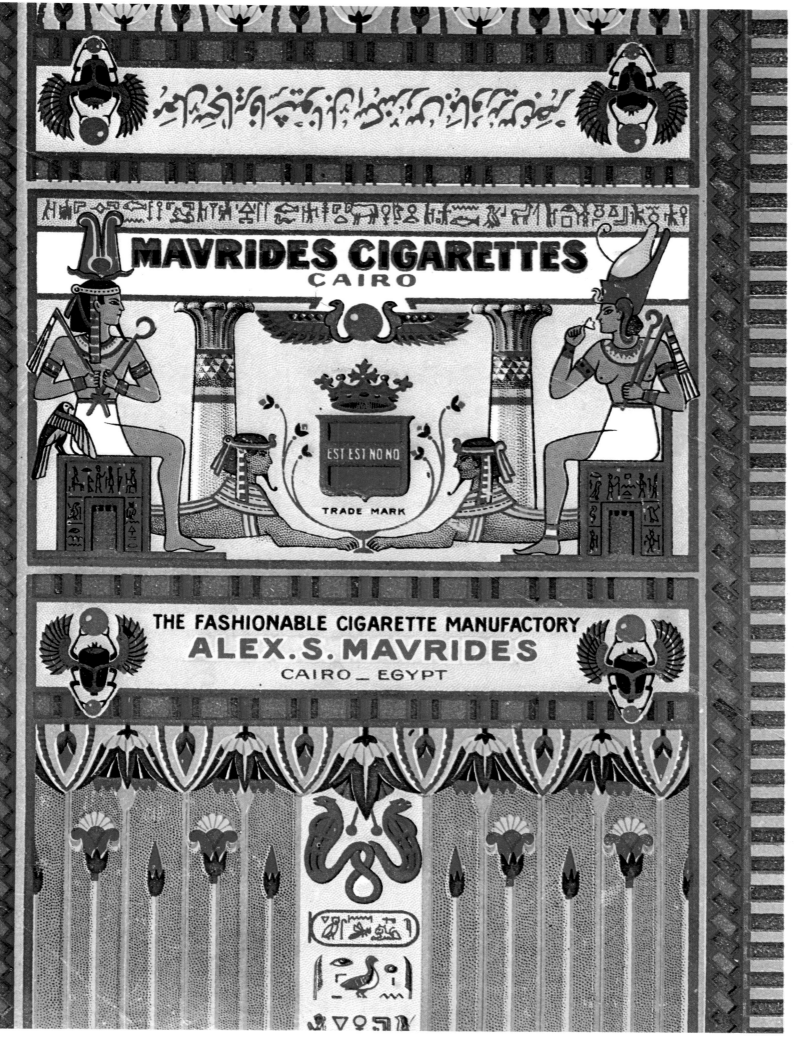

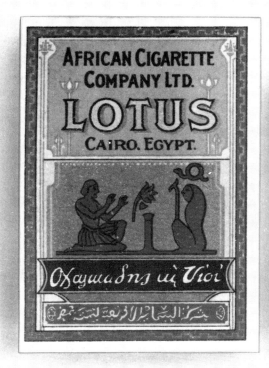

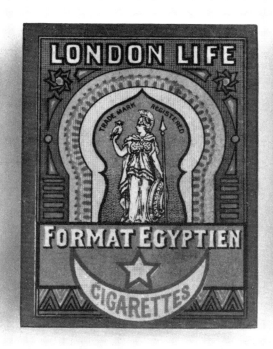

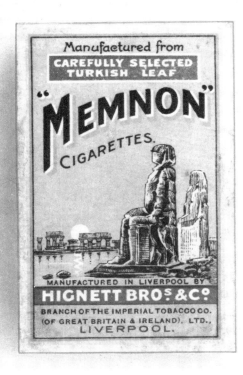

Visions of the East

When American or British packs were designed for the home market by industrially trained artists whose brief was 'do me something Egyptian', they quite often took short cuts.

Some confusion is evident in the African Cigarette Company's *Lotus* cigarette (UK, dated 1908) where, in a delightfully balanced design, the brand name is emphasized by two strange, isolated mythic figures who are throwing a lotus leaf over a primitive tennis net. Hignett's *Memnon* cigarettes (UK, dated 1909) shows the statue of Amenhotep III at Thebes, associated with Memnon by the Greeks. The statue was meant to give out a strange musical note when touched by the rising sun at dawn, an odd story to support a cigarette promotion. Increasing the confusion, the phrase, 'manufactured from carefully selected Turkish leaf' is printed prominently on both sides.

One pack shows the ultimate crime – the capture of Britannia by the wily exotics. In *London Life* cigarettes, *Format Egyptien*, Britannia, the white robed symbol of British fortitude, finds herself confined in a series of interlocking Islamic arches, pierced at the corners to give the effect of lattice screens. In case you have just found your footing, the designer has balanced the whole structure on a star and crescent moon, an emblem of Turkey.

Lloyd's *Go Bang* (UK, on sale in 1896; the 5 pack shown here was printed by Tillotson & Son of Bolton and Liverpool) is about as warped a vision of the East as you will find on a Western pack. The restricted range of bright colours and the simple drawing style are the sure sign of Comic influence. Presumably the little fellow has not yet been told the brand name. It is not one that would survive in the Age of the bland brand name. Neither could you expect to see today such a juxtaposition as the Morris' *Rhodesia* pack of the 1930s that has the brand name casually floating over the Pyramids.

American firms too could take short cuts. Shown below are three well-known brands, *Egyptian Mysteries* (1923, Coulapides, box of 20), *Egyptienne Straights* (1898, Butler-Butler, and later the American Tobacco Company; shown here a box 20), and the famous *Mogul* brand (1904, started by Anargyros, and after 1911, one of the large range of Turkish exotics including *Murad* that was ceded to Lorillard).

The *Egyptienne Straights* pack features an Assyrian Winged Bull that stands on a plinth with the usual ludicrous hieroglyphs derived from feathers, exclamation marks and musical notation, headed by a bird staring at the sun out to sea. The *Egyptian Mysteries* design exploits a bizarre blend of religious ceremony and flagellation, not in itself unusual, but here plainly ridiculous.

The *Mogul* Egyptian cigarette 'made from selected Turkish Tobaccos' was a celebrated brand of the hey-day of the Turkish cigarette. They were extensively, and beautifully advertised, and were associated with their slogan, 'Just like being in Cairo'. Oddly, for an Egyptian cigarette made from Turkish tobaccos, the design features a turbanned ruler, perhaps the Emperor of Delhi himself, the Great Mogul, casually smoking near his Palace.

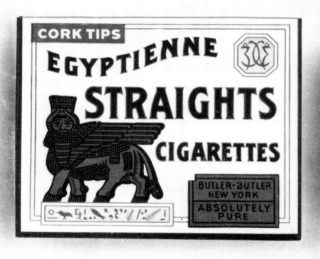

The Tartars

Ironically, considering the fact that in earlier centuries the death sentence had been imposed for the smoking of tobacco in Russia, the Russian cigarette became synonymous with luxury living – rich, dark heady tobacco, often wrapped in black paper with a long gold-covered tip. One boy recorded in Paul Thompson's *The Edwardians* would go through his parents' pockets when they came home drunk, buy cakes and cigarettes for his gang, 'we'd go

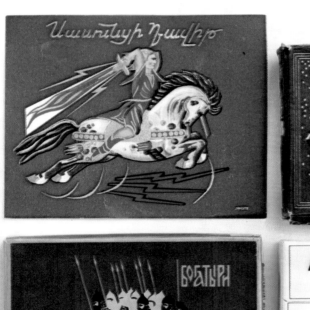

along like lords along the river, puffing away these fancy Russian cigarettes, red-tipped ones, gold-tipped, and have a good feed.' As early as 1850 the La Ferme factory in St Petersburg was blending Turkish and American tobaccos for the domestic trade. These skills spread west as many British and American factories employed hundreds of Russian *émigrés* as cigarette rollers before the introduction of machinery. The Russian connection is reflected in many of the early American brand names, in Bedrossian's *Alexandrevicz*, *Moscow* and *St Petersburg* for instance. After the 1917 Revolution the Russian cigarette continued to be produced in the West, as many of the manufacturers

set up business in exile, notably in Denmark.

On Russian post-Revolutionary packs the old aristocratic images of Tsarist coats-of-arms and heraldic beasts are discarded, and instead we see, for example, industrial and agricultural workers, their horses and cows, all smoking *Mosselprom* cigarettes (about 1925, see Bojko, *New Graphic Design in Revolutionary Russia* 1972).

Many of the USSR's cigarette packs for domestic consumption are less glossy and fanciful than contemporary Western packs. They express achievements rather than associations; you find packs featuring industrial projects, electricity workers and factory workers. They are probably the only brands that consistently feature the people who smoke them, albeit idealized and always staring into the sun. The *Woodbine* design tends to hedge the issue compared with one Russian pack that shows a miner, lamp in hat, drill over shoulder, standing resolutely at the pit-head, with a coal tip in the distance.

The lack of advertising images helping to project the brands is perhaps compensated for by the national enthusiasm for the commemorative special issue, celebrating the 50th Anniversary of the Revolution, the launching of the Sputnik, and dogs in

space. In 1975 Philip Morris Inc, USA and Glavtabak, USSR brought out the Apollo-Soyuz American blend cigarette to celebrate the joint USA-USSR space mission. The brand was made at the Yava Factory in Moscow with a blend of 75% American to 25% domestic tobaccos, incorporating an American filter. Whereas the packs disappeared virtually overnight in Moscow, they were too expensive and too unusual to catch on in any great way in America.

Brands exported from the USSR do not tend to celebrate technological advances. The rest of the world's received image is of the pre-Revolutionary period, resurrected in richly coloured, sophisticated flat boxes.

The three most visually appealing of these export packs feature horsemen. The colour effect and printing techniques on the galloping swordsperson pack is rich almost to the point of enamelling. Great blocks of opaque colour are used on the *Bogatyry* (meaning 'elder hero') flat box lid, a stylized grouping of medieval knights with lances, in the spirit of Eisenstein's film *Alexander Nevsky*. The last pack is a box of *Troika*, a more inventive and appealing design, of a three-horsed decorated sled pulling two elderly men through the winter landscape.

CHAPTER SEVEN

THE GREAT OUTDOORS

Many of the most stylish and exciting packs respond to the call of the wild, the wide open spaces, the colour and pattern of unspoilt nature. To counter claims that cigarettes were unhealthy and unsociable, packs presented a gallery of Outdoor Heroes, football and baseball players, cyclists and racing drivers, cowboys and indians. Even animals and birds contributed.

Man in the Landscape

Cigarettes have long been associated with the Great Outdoors, despite the fact that they are chiefly smoked indoors or at least in restricted places. Some of the earliest images associated with cigarette packs concerned the enjoyment of the open air, the evocation of the sweeping landscape and, particularly, the active participation in sports.

The Countryside

Both *Beechwood* (UK, about 1930) and Lloyd's *Big Tree* (UK, 1935) offer to the smoker the lure of the leafy forest glade. Neither pack is seen to be populated by other smokers or tourists. Both present a rustic seclusion with healthy living and dappled light, a celebration of the British countryside that appeals to both the romantic and the patriot, offering that great intangible so beloved of the advertising man, 'Freedom'. The *Beechwood* pack, here shown in its two sizes, 10 and 20, 'Well matured in Bond to eliminate all Harshness', deserves greater study. It was a brand marketed by the Cooperative Wholesale Society, a trading federation of English stores founded in 1863. The design combines a landscape scene with two bands of decoration best described as austere Art Deco, the last remnants of Sunburst and Aztec styles.

However, the cigarette was essentially a creature of the twentieth century, and the pack had also to express the activities and enthusiasms of twentieth century, primarily urban, populations; registering man's presence in the landscape in a more dynamic way than shown, for instance on the front of the Corsican brand *Mistral*.

Motoring

Wills' *Autocar* was registered as a trademark for the French market, which actually meant for the French colonial market, in 1908. Like many of the British-American Tobacco packs destined for areas with many different dialects and languages, the image had to be simple and immediately recognizable. The motor car was, in the period before the Great War, synonymous with speed, daring and spectacle. The writer CFG Masterman saw them in the lanes of England 'wandering machines racing with incredible velocity and no apparent aim'. At the time this pack was produced the mass production of autocars was still in its infancy. In 1904 there were only about

8,500 motorcars in England. Imagine then the impact on the French colonies, as a vision of what was happening at the seat of Empire. Other foreign smokers may have noticed the similarity between Wills' *Autocar* and the design of the American brand *Motor*, launched by 'Buck' Duke in 1897.

The pack itself, in subtly blended shades of olive and pale bottle green, shows a demonic surge of violent action worthy of the Italian Futurist painters. The English Futurist CRW Nevinson was later to sculpt an *Automobilist* or machine slave, stressing the sinister robot driver, made threatening and anonymous in his thick travelling coat. Wills' *Autocar* is an extraordinary image of speed – this is no domestic

airing in the landscape. Perhaps it can be seen as an early manifestation of that link between smoking and motor sport, culminating in the sponsorship of that sport by the tobacco companies. The Autocar does seem to be going faster than the compulsory speed limit of 20mph. It is just possible that we are spectators to one of the early motor races. The sport was forbidden on road circuits at this date. The design of the pack heightens the impact of the event, the maker's name almost as legible as a car's registration plate, and almost in the correct position. The two horizontal panels simply frame the prime feature, which, with its elliptical sides, may suggest that we are catching sight of the Autocar through our own rear-view mirror. This would mean that we are about to be overtaken by this smoking, shuddering vision of technological advance as it hurtles through the calm and peaceful British countryside.

The imagery of motoring on packs becomes less frenetic after the First World War. The car became less of a novelty. The design of the *Motor* cigarette label (page 74) shows how refined the activity had become. Other motoring packs of the Twenties and Thirties have the motorist stopped at the roadside, lighting a cigarette, calm and relaxed, linking the image with the smoke of cigarettes rather than the smoke of exhaust.

Sporting Activities

This is of course only one use of the theme of Man (and it is very rarely a woman) in the landscape. Dwarfing all other fresh air subjects is that of Sport, the energetic but friendly rivalry in the open landscape, sharpened but also tempered by good fellowship and *bonhomie*. Today's cigarette advertisements tend to avoid the sort of heroic feats you might see on yesterday's Sports packs (see overleaf). Instead they stress vehicle sports, scrambling, motor racing, where the emphasis is less on human being than machine.

The Edwardian Superstar of the Sports field is magnificently portrayed on BAT's *Rugby* (about 1910). On the back, a section of the game is revealed, as the red shirts rush in to score a try. On the front, the gentleman player, despite the sheer weight of his clothing, kicks the ball so hard it shoots straight out of the pack. This extraordinary figure is drawn with a primitive zest worthy of Henri Rousseau.

Edwards, Ringer & Bigg's *League* cigarettes cunningly double their potential clientele by combining the emblems of the local Rugby Football Club with those of the nearby Bristol Soccer Club. On the front of the pack, using an inventive split screen technique, the two sports are again featured with dynamic all-action shots of the respective sportsmen, many adopting that curious pose (first seen in *Rugby*) of the arms held close to the chest as the legs propel the body about.

To show how widespread was the appeal to the sporting spirit, overleaf you will find just a small selection of Sport Packs from all over the world, from the UK *Foursome, Sport, Sportsman, Polo* (from both Ogden's and Murray's), and *Cycle;* from Holland *Toss;* from Norway *Knockout;* from the USA *Homerun* and *Cycle* (Liggett & Myers), and a *Sports* (unidentified).

Smoking in the Open Air

This subject cannot be left without a word on the several attempts by cigarette manufacturers to face and overcome some of the difficulties encountered by the Outdoor Smoker. Think how unsightly is the cigarette that has burned unevenly because of the prevailing wind, the charred cusp of unburnt paper, the furiously incinerating tip. Neither is it particularly comfortable to smoke in the rain.

An anonymous American company produced the *Eagle Wet Proof* cigarette, 'Smoke in the rain – even if your fingers are wet'. It was perhaps the difficulty of lighting the cigarette in the wind that led to the *Self-Lighting Cigarette*. Rather than use a match the smoker merely rubbed the red spot at the end of the cigarette against the striking surface on the pack side, and if all went well, the red spot flamed, igniting the cigarette. On the pack, the company recommended that the smoker wait a few seconds before inhaling, to allow certain gases to disperse. This technological marvel was abandoned at the end of the 1960s because of consumer resistance and the danger to health.

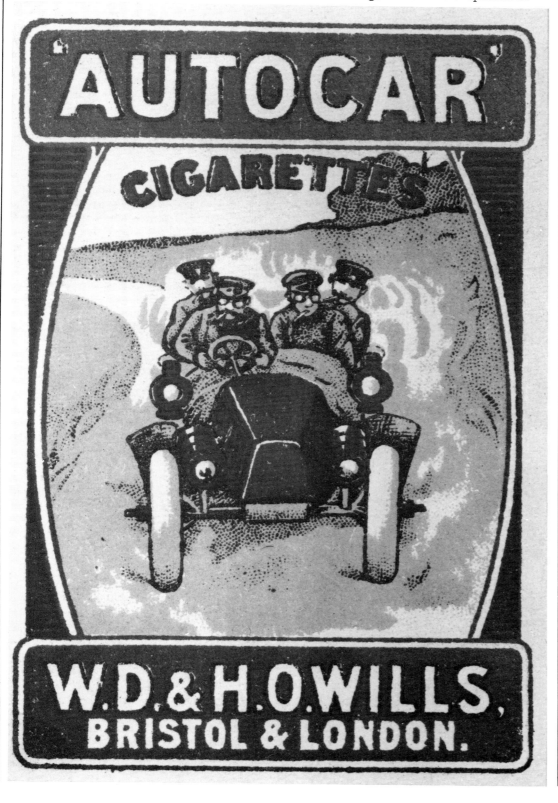

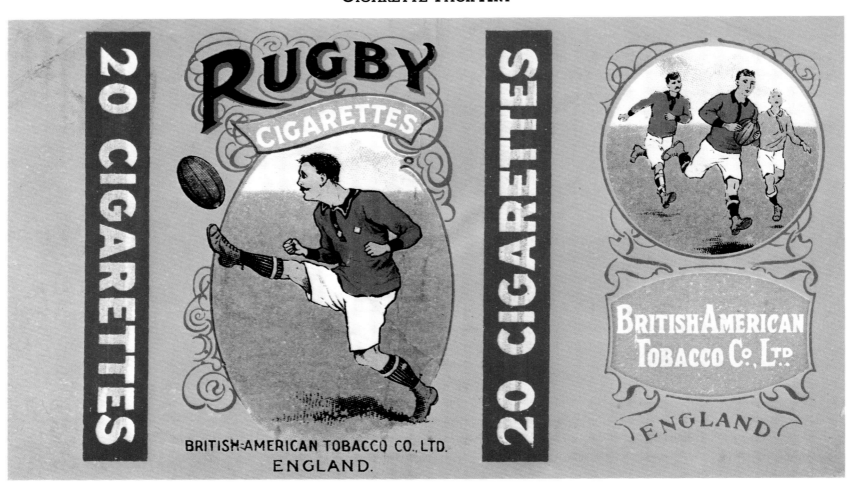

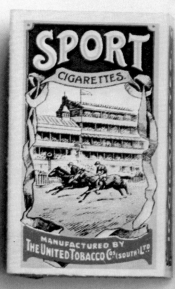

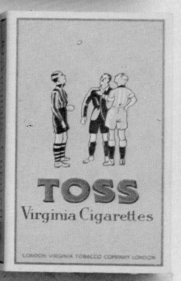

The Call of the Wild

'With the smoke of a Lucky Strike curling upwards, a man can dream of Pocahontas in her garden at Varina, of settlers farming with holstered pistols on the handles of their ploughs . . .' (Roy Flanagan *The Story of Lucky Strike)*.

Cowboys and Indians

The imagery of the past and the life of adventure are necessary ingredients in the promotion of the cigarette. In American cigarette mythology, two figures loom large, the Indian and the Frontiersman. The Indian has done sterling service on tobacco packaging ever since the nineteenth century. His romanticized image reminds Americans of the days of the early settlers, of the Virginia colony whose success was based on tobacco cultivation. Much of the planter's expertise was learnt at first hand from Indians such as Powhatan, chief of the Virginian Indians, who appears on the American Tobacco Company's *111* brand. Powhatan was the father of the legendary Pocahontas. Most American tobacconists at the turn of the nineteenth century celebrated this historic connection with carved, or even cast figures of Indian braves who guarded their shop fronts.

A much more recent example is this export pack from Colombia, which offers American smokers a stylized, elegant version of their national image.

The cowboy, by comparison, has inspired fewer pack fronts but recently Marlboro has used him by association with its advertising campaigns. A version distributed to the British Empire, from a similar world of moral absolutes and intimate contact with nature, is Wills' *Rough Rider* pack, an export brand depicting, in fact, one of Teddy Roosevelt's 1st Volunteer Cavalry in the Spanish-American War of 1898, but suggesting pioneer life everywhere. The pack is still on sale in Malaysia today.

Of greater attraction has been the *Bandit*, the figure that has traditionally sent a thrill down the reader's or the traveller's spine. In their pack of 5 cigarettes (with holder, about 1905), Lambert & Butler have employed a stage bandit bedecked in fancy waistcoat, head scarf and cummerbund, rather delicately counting his money perhaps, while on the back of the pack is wealth beyond his dreams, the huge range of medals, coins and awards

LAMBERT & BUTLER'S "Bandit" Cigarettes With Holder.

won by the company. Opposite you'll see Malaysia's *Zorro* ('absolutely harmless to the throat') presenting a much more formidable spectacle, leather-gloved and masked, the Goddess of Pleasure and Pain, advancing on the smoker with singing whip and flared nostrils.

The Boy Scout

The European smoker had few images to rival the American wild men. The exotic Spanish cigarette girl was not really adequate. One variation on the cowboy is provided by the Boy Scout, an institutionalized and licensed cowboy. The two packs here seem a calculated snub to the movement. Baden-Powell wrote, 'A scout does not smoke because he is not such a fool. I have no opinion of cigarettes – they are what women and little boys smoke . . . Cigarettes are to my mind the smoke of the herd, of fidgety, flighty people . . .' Yet, despite his contempt, here are two Boy Scouts puffing away. The Malayan pack *Boy-Scout* (about 1930) has even printed on it 'A British Empire Product'. Consistent with Baden-Powell's prejudices about the Latin races, on the *Cheftain Boys Scout's Cigarettes* (sic, about 1930, French colonies), the scout is not only smoking, but doing it with great panache, not to say suspicious affectation.

Animal Imagery

Cigarette manufacturers have a particular fondness for animals in all shapes and sizes. To close the chapter, there is on the following page a selection of packs from all over the world that feature these innocents.

From China, there is *Flying Horse*, *Golden Horse*, *Dog's Head*, *Golden Sparrow* and *Elephant*, with the Revolutionary panda pack *Xiongmao*. From India comes *Bat*, from Canada *Mallard*, from Britain *Robin*, *Tiger*, *White Swans* and *Golden Butterfly*, from Japan the *Glory* pack commemorating the coronation of the Emperor Hirohito, and from Malaya, *Three Geese*, with a Bear's *Teddy Bear* to complete the picture.

The images of animals on packs seem to fall into two categories, the first a simple image for instant product identification, and the second, a celebration of unspoilt innocent Nature.

Of the first group the most impressive is surely Lloyd's *Tiger* (about 1920, export pack), staring out from the central circular panel. There is no attempt to show natural lair, prey or habitat. It concentrates on the extraordinarily powerful contours of the face, the regal glare against the intense blue background.

Less regal is the pre-war Chinese pack *Dog's Head*, from the Capitol Cigarette Company, Shanghai, that shows a fierce, liverish bull-dog with an almost human truculence in its expression, yet carefully drawn with a restraining collar. Both this pack and *Elephant* (China, Union Cigarette Co) were produced in pre-Revolutionary China, and, such was the number of languages and dialects spoken in the various provinces, they really constitute export packs. The *Robin* pack was also intended for export (Ogden's, pack dated 1905), a bright note of black and red set against a winter landscape. The lettering of the brand name takes up this note – each letter has a black back and a red breast. The Chinese pack *Golden Sparrow*, seems to show its influence.

But it is the pictures of animals in landscapes that are the most satisfying aesthetically, and certainly more demanding of the artist and printer. The basic theme is that of the open air, unpolluted by the city, where animals can be seen in their native habitat, the complete antithesis of urban smoking. Visually there was no danger of creating damaging references to class, creed or colour, and the pack might charm everyone. In the case of Thos Bear & Sons' *Teddy Bear* cigarettes, exported

widely throughout the 1920s and beyond, the image of the animal was there not only as a play on the maker's name, but also perhaps as a visual delight for the children in the community, a concept that would not be at all possible today.

At times then, we see the animals at rest, serenely oblivious to our presence, such as the *White Swans* (UK, United Tobacco Co) and their very near relatives, visually speaking, *Three Geese* from Malaysia, that float so calmly down stream. The *Xiongmao* pandas peacefully munch bamboo shoots in domestic contentment, at a picnic in the mountains.

At other times the packs radiate an extraordinary sense of energy, of animals moving through the elements, the dramatic silhouette of the *Bat* against the moon, the clarion call of the cockerel against the full blaze of the sun in *Glory*, the rising form of the *Mallard*, the *Golden Horse* running along the skyline. The most dynamic of these packs is the *Flying Horse*, where the animal's power takes it clear of land and city, like some latter-day Pegasus. It is fair to say that *Mosselprom* excepted (see page 82), no animal is seen actually smoking. There is perhaps one further exception, the Australian brand *Kookaburra*, where a couple of furtive birds are seen in the trees, guiltily puffing away at their cigarettes.

10 CIGARETTES

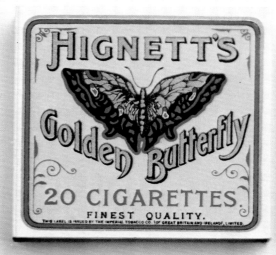

CHAPTER EIGHT

ADVERTISING THE PACK

The period between the Wars was an age of intense and often unscrupulous advertising, as the cigarette industry flourished all over the world. Pack design became more lean and considered under the influence of the newly emerging science of market research. The whole industry was to change in the 1940s, with the introduction of the king-size and filter-tip.

Brand Rivalries between the Wars

With due apologies to other companies, it is possible to see cigarette promotions of the 1920s and 1930s in America as a three-horse race between Reynolds' *Camel*, American Tobacco's *Lucky Strike* and Liggett & Myers' *Chesterfield*. Time and time again one would surge ahead, the other two responding with more intensive advertising campaigns and promotional devices. While Liggett & Myers' *Chesterfield* stuck resolutely to 'They Satisfy' and, in 1931, 'Blow some my way', *Camel* and *Lucky Strike* tried a variety of new approaches.

In 1924 the *Lucky* ad ran 'Forty Five Minutes Toasting develops its Aristocratic Flavor – the Enormous production makes possible its democratic price.' And when *Camel* mocked, 'It's Fun to be Fooled', GW Hill hit back with 'Your Throat Protection – against Irritation – against Cough', implying on other occasions the existence of several strange impurities in his competitors' brands, including sheep dip.

In 1931 *Lucky Strike* and *Camel* were offering the new Humidor pack, *Camel*, 'Smoke a Fresh Cigarette', and 'Zip – and its open!', (*Lucky Strike*, during the Talking Cigarette campaign). By this time Camel were establishing a homely style of advertising, 'Watch those Camels, Peg . . .' (1930 advertisement). *Lucky Strike* tried something more obvious, '20,679 Physicians say Luckies are *less irritating*', in their 1930 campaign.

Precious!
"Watch those Camels, Peg. They're nine-tenths of the vacation."

Don't deny yourself the luxury of

Camels

A particularly amusing campaign mounted by Hill was the 'Reach for a Lucky instead of a Sweet', in 1928. One invidious example of the genre showed a slim young horsewoman leaping a fence on her sleek chestnut horse, while a huge purple coloured whale of a woman is unable to get her horse over the obstacle, 'Pretty Curves Win'.

As well as advertisements both companies used the new and powerful medium of radio. *Lucky Strike* used the airwaves first with the Lucky Strike Radio Hour, and ran the Lucky Strike Dance Orchestra. *Camel* answered with Morton Downey and Tony Wons and the Camel Quarter Hour. *Chesterfield* signed up Bing Crosby who, according to a recent interview shortly before his death, was subsequently sacked for refusing to say on the air, 'Don't forget to buy your Mother a carton of *Chesterfield* on Mother Day', as his mother was an ardent non-smoker.

The Ten-Centers

Despite the vast financial resources of the big cigarette companies, the years of the Depression, the years from 1929 to 1932, were dangerous times. By the end of 1932, 20% of the US cigarette market was occupied by the 'ten-centers', new ten cent packs, as sales of the previously dominant fifteen cent packs dropped by 10,000 million. There was an equivalent rise in the consumption of the Roll Your Own tobaccos. (*Bull Durham's* slogan was 'Roll your own and save your roll.')

In September 1931 WT Reed of Larus & Brother Co brought out *White Rolls* at 10 cents for 20. In November that year Philip Morris reduced their *Paul Jones* to 10 cents, and in March 1932 Brown & Williamson's *Wings* was reduced in price to compete. In June 1932 the fourth major ten-center was launched, Axton Fisher's *Twenty Grand*.

The ten-center offered a cheaper product because of the fall in leaf prices, and sensible economies in advertising and packaging. According to *Fortune* magazine, November 1932, Brown & Williamson said, 'cut out the ballyhoo and fancy packing, and let the public have what it wants, a good smoke. You can't smoke cellophane.' Some of these cheaper packs are reproduced on page 93.

Survival of the Big Three

The 'Big Three' brands of course survived the ten-centers. They were joined by two other successful brands, Lorillard's *Old Gold* (1926) and *Philip*

Morris (1933). The advertising battle intensified.

Among other notable campaigns, *Lucky Strike* had a burning cigarette that spoke in its smoke, 'I am your Lucky Strike, I am your best friend. Try me. I'll never let you down.' *Camel* used personal endorsements from such stars as champion skater Jack Shea, 'To relieve fatigue – get a lift with a Camel. Naturally I feel pretty well used up after the last hard sprint to the tape. Camels restore my "pep", the "lifting effect" is noticeable in a very few minutes and they taste so good.' *Old Gold* ran a series of drawings of the Petty Girls, lissom lovelies recovering their peace of mind, 'Shanghaied by a silly salt . . . offer him an Old Gold . . . he'll welcome it like a breeze in the doldrums . . . while you breeze gracefully away.' *Philip Morris*, introduced in 1933, was probably the most successful new brand of the decade. Some older packs survived, such as *Old Mill*, which despite its appearance was still going in 1943.

Perhaps American design of the 1930s lacked the vigour and excitement of the Twenties' packs, the *Clown* pack, the *Wooden Kimona Nails*. Something of the spirit of *The Blue Horse Pills* survives in Brown & Williamson's *Penguin*, a menthol brand of 1931. But the old style seems to be waning in Philip Morris' *Barking Dog* of 1938. Despite the brand name the dog seems to be either bored or reflecting on his lot. The future of pack design lay with the chevron and stripe patterns of *Zephyr* (Brown & Williamson, 1938). One extravagance of the 1930s was Axton Fisher's *Head Play*, an 11 inch cigarette that took advantage of a tax loophole. This was a typical piece of adventurism by Woodford Fitch Axton, owner of the largest privately controlled cigarette company in America. Colonel Axton's major brand of the 1930s was *Spud*, which he had bought in 1926 from Lloyd 'Spud' Hughes of Mingo Junction, Ohio. Hughes had found a way of blending menthol and tobacco. The Colonel increased production and marketed the product nationally, 'Your mouth keeps fresh as April if you keep to *Spuds*.' 'Spud' Hughes used his new fortune to open an airport. He entered air races, beginning a long series of expensive and ultimately ruinous crashes, the most spectacular of which occurred when, returning from the Cleveland air races, he tried to land by the light of a pocket torch. By 1928 he was broke, working at a filling station and devising a new mint julep cigarette.

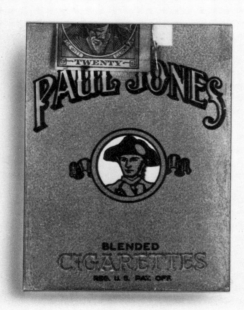

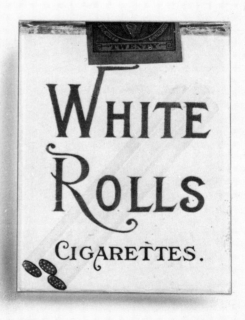

Unsolicited Testimonials

One of the major innovations of the advertising campaigns between the wars was the use of figures from the entertainment world, film stars, crooners and jazz musicians. It is particularly noticeable that women are used in this capacity for the first time.

Let's look specifically at *Lucky Strike's* contributions. Virginia Cross of Anniston, Alabama advised the American public, 'Consider your Adam's Apple', as a large white arrow jabbed mercilessly at her throat. This was not an anti-smoking advertisement but a suggestion that you switch to *Luckies*. 'Don't rasp your throat with harsh irritants . . . reach for a Lucky instead.' (1931). A well known operatic soprano was persuaded to endorse a brand, a campaign that anticipated recent sponsorships of the performing arts in Britain by the tobacco companies.

But *Lucky Strike* particularly favoured actresses, women who had created separate careers, and were slim enough to qualify under the *Lucky* slogan 'Reach for a Lucky instead of a Sweet.' Some advertisements, like the Dorothy Mackail endorsement, widely printed in 1931, offered joint publicity. 'Watch for Dorothy in her next First National Picture *Safe in Hell*. There is never a dull moment in any of the First National's pictures starring that Mackail girl.' Miss Mackail replies, 'Give me Lucky Strike every time.' The mutual benefits were obliquely referred to in the small print, 'You may be interested in knowing that not one cent was paid to Miss Mackail to make the above statement. Miss Mackail has been a smoker of Lucky Strike cigarettes for six years.'

Under the caption 'Cream of the Crop' we find in Lucky ads of the 1930s stars such as Douglas Fairbanks Jr ('Doug has stuck to Luckies for four years, but didn't stick the makers of Luckies anything for his kind words. You're a brick, Doug.') and Helen Twelvetrees. Where Doug's frame bears attributes of his life-style, Helen Twelvetrees, star of 'Panama Flo', has a vanity ribbon over her head and supporting wreath.

Little of the glamour, romance, chicanery and foolishness that marked American design for the cigarette industry ever crossed the Atlantic to enliven the newspapers and hoardings of the European markets.

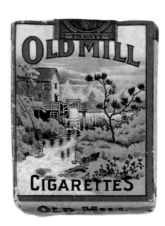

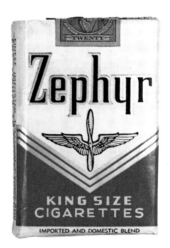

Britain and the Coupon War of the Thirties

The major British brands that fought for market supremacy at the beginning of the 1930s were familiar enough names. *Woodbine*, *Weights* and *Park Drive* were the combatants in the cheap range. In the middle were Player's *Navy Cut*, *Gold Flake* and *Capstan*. Carreras' *Craven A*, launched in 1921, was making great headway here. The best-sellers in the more expensive brands were *Passing Clouds* and *Three Castles*.

The style of advertising was gentlemanly. It was rumoured that *Gold Flake* had a peculiar sort of nip that irritated the smoker's throat. *Craven A* capitalized on the rumour with nothing more aggressive than 'Craven A does not harm the throat'. We are a long way from suggestions that competitors' brands are polluted with sheep dip.

In the late 1920s the new radio stars were signed up for testimonials, Peter Dawson and Henry Hall, Gilly Potter and Peggy Cochrane. Film stars such as Binnie Barnes and Jack Hulbert were seen in publicity campaigns for Wills' cigarettes that also plugged their latest films.

In 1927 the American Tobacco Company entered the British market with the acquisition of Wix' Company and their most celebrated brand *Kensitas* (see page 72), but little of GW Hill's abrasive advertising style was seen in London.

The cause of turbulence in the cigarette industry was not the spectacular introduction of new brands, but the economic effects of the Depression. Whereas American companies responded to economic collapse and stagnation by reducing prices, British companies were drawn into a bitter and uncompromising Coupon War.

Carreras had operated a flourishing trade in coupon cigarettes for years with their *Black Cat*, from a safe independent position outside the Imperial Tobacco Company, which did not approve of such vulgarity. In 1930 Wix (American Tobacco Company) turned *Kensitas* into a coupon brand. Battle was joined by competitors offering a mass of gifts and bonuses. By 1931 there were altogether twenty-two current coupon schemes in Britain. Far from looking on with typical British reserve, smokers threw themselves wholeheartedly into these schemes. For many people the gifts were not just novelties, but, during a

period of hardship, a valuable source of household necessities such as clothing and razors.

Wills' only response to the prevailing anarchy was to launch a scheme for exchanging complete series of cigarette cards for reproductions of such paintings as FD Millet's *Between Two Fires* and JE Millais' *The Boyhood of Raleigh*. But soon the position was so serious that they capitulated and, in 1932, brought out a coupon brand, *Four Aces*, at 5 for 2d, but also selling in 10 packs. The pack front features familiar themes, luck and gambling, perhaps suitable to the atmosphere of the times. Within twelve months *Four Aces* had captured 22% of the coupon trade.

Although there were undoubted benefits for successful coupon brands, there were also logistic difficulties.

Whole new departments had to be set up to receive and check coupon claims. The public learnt fast how to short-circuit the schemes with such tricks as submitting a pack of vouchers the right size and weight that turned out to be a fast-melting pack of butter. A truce, in the form of an agreement by the big companies, ended the Coupon War, with large compensation for the firms that suffered. Everybody sighed with relief.

Among the now familiar brands launched in Britain in the pre-war period were Lambert & Butler's *Matinée* (1938), Jackson's *du Maurier* (1929, and a pioneer of the move to filters,) and Rothman's *Consulate* (1938, and the first major brand in the British menthol range), together typical of the stylish geometrical packing fashionable in the 1930s.

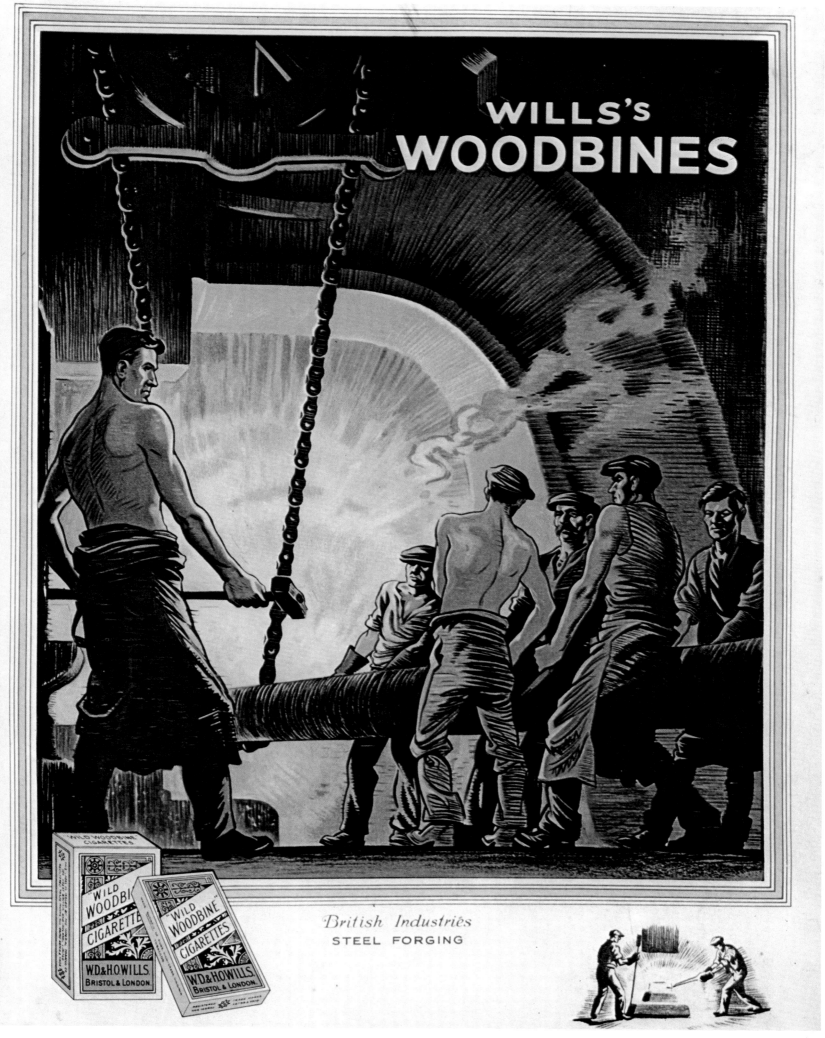

British Industries
STEEL FORGING

The Showcard

The cigarette pack was only one of many devices used to promote or reinforce the product. In eras of intense competition such as the 1890s and 1930s great emphasis was placed on advertising on the tradesman's premises – enamel signs on the outside, such as those shown here, the pelmet flash to the top of door or window, the window transparency, the counter card that has to be small enough to sit on the counter yet be attractive enough to catch the eye, and, hanging at the back of a window display, or somewhere on the walls of the crowded shop, the showcard. As a writer in 1897 wrote, these cards had to be of the best quality 'in these days when brands are infinite in number, while the tobacconist's wall and window space is exceedingly limited in area, causing the good man to select only the best for display.'

For loyal and prestigious retailers cigarette companies would have printed showcards of exceptional quality, specially framed and glazed. The Player's showcard of about 1900 (page 23) is in this category. It shows not only the firm's range of products but also the grandiose vision of the scale of their operations.

Wills seem to have favoured series of showcards. The example reproduced here is one of the 1935 series, 'The Men who smoke Woodbines'. It represents steel-forging, and is typical of the way in which *Woodbine* was promoted, a cigarette smoked by ordinary people, yet part of the heroism of modern life. The brand is sold in exactly the same way today, 'No nonsense. No airs. Like Woodbine. Like you.' runs the terse copy, over the gritty, grizzled mechanic or factory worker.

Printing and preparing showcards was an important part of any printing company's services offered to the tobacco industry. In 1897 the correspondent of *Tobacco* magazine recorded the existence of a flourishing showcard and novelty department at Mardon, Son & Hall of Bristol. He particularly admired a portrait of Queen Victoria, surrounded by the cigarette cards series 'Kings and Queens of England', a special presentation feature to celebrate the Diamond Jubilee. Proof prints were taken on silk for Mardon's own festivities, 'and they had the honour of receiving an order from the Queen for a number of copies.' Many more prints were ordered by the Royal Family.

While not needing the permanent surface of the enamel plate, the showcard, because of its exposure to direct sunlight in the window, had to have fast colours. Because of the risk of accidents or graffiti, the surface of the card had to be washable. The printed card would be delivered from the lithographic department, and each front would be treated manually with a semi-liquid, clear, gelatine-like substance known to the irreverent as 'tacky', and made from the firm's own invention, the 'Mardozene Tablet', a compound whose ingredients were shrouded in secrecy.

After the long and crucial processes of drying, the cards were taken to the mounting and framing department, where machines edged them with metal and fixed what the trade called suspenders to the back, fittings of metal hooks and string. Each card was further strengthened by a backing of calico glued on by a staff of girls – 'the extent of their operations may be gauged by the size of the glue pot at their command. A hundredweight is a trifle in its capacious maw . . .'

With the decline of the small shop showcards have largely fallen out of favour, and the rare examples that exist today rely heavily on themes developed on radio and television.

"Black Cat"

Pure Matured
Virginia Cigarettes

China and Japan between the Wars

By a lucky chance, a small collection of Chinese cigarette packs dating from before the Second World War has survived in excellent condition. Apart from those shown here, others can be found on pages 65, 76 and 90.

Both China and Japan were importing tobacco by the seventeenth century to such an extent that the Shogun of Japan arrested a hundred and fifty people for trafficking in the weed. Thirteen years after, in 1644, the Emperor of China ordered massive stores of tobacco destroyed.

At the beginning of the twentieth century the Chinese market had been cultivated, even dominated, by 'Buck' Duke's American Tobacco Company, and his agent Jim Thomas. After the formation of British-American Tobacco, China became that company's greatest market.

Western Firms in the Far East

In Japan 'Buck' Duke bought a well-established tobacco firm, the Mural Brothers, and ran it under the powerful supervision of Edward J Parrish. Parrish observed that Japanese smokers preferred the milder tobaccos, 'as they prefer milder food.' Mural sold *Old Gold*, *Cycle* and *Piedmont*, using an abrasive, bouncy style of advertising. In a newspaper photograph of the time, a crowd, brandishing aloft a 10 foot pack of *Pin Head* cigarettes, demonstrates on behalf of Duke's products. Eventually the Mural firm was taken over when the Japanese government established a tobacco monopoly.

The dominance of the Far East markets by Western firms probably meant that the packaging, too, was planned and printed in the West. Certainly the *Golden Sunshade* pack, exported by Ogden's of Britain to China (10 finest cigarettes, about 1935), is consistent with that firm's house style – the girl could almost be in fancy dress, and her extremely stylized sunshade bears little resemblance to the delicate structures and colouring of the Chinese original. An interesting touch of elaboration, you'll notice that while she keeps her jacket on, she has changed her skirt for the other side of the pack. The word 'Golden' appears on several of these packs, *Horse*, *Sparrow*, *Sunshade* and *Dragon*. Perhaps they are the Chinese equivalent of the British Gold Flake cigarettes.

Packs Produced in China

However, from certain clues it may be possible to distinguish packs with a clearer Chinese identity. Many of the 1930s packs introduced here have a heaviness and opacity of colour that is not found on Western packs of the time – the dense reds and blues of *Hwan Ying* (10 selected cigarettes, British Cigarette Co Ltd) and the rich green, red and blue on *Flywheel* (10, Nanyang Brothers).

What images, then, do we find on the packs that represent the product? We have a standard pin-up pack, *Chi Mai* (10 cigarettes, Tuck Loong, Shanghai), with a shy, hesitant beauty who dares not look us in the eye. In *Flywheel* we have the deification of technology with the flywheel itself borne aloft on heavenly wings set in heavenly mandorla. *Hwan Ying* offers an oriental version of the Easy Life, a stately home in the country seen through imposing gates. Despite appearances, we assume it's not a hospital. In *Daffodil* (10, Man Ching

Cigarette Co), the tang of the open air, the processes of natural growth are again used to persuade us that we must smoke. For the front, the artist has chosen a naturalistic treatment for the bunch of daffodils, while on the back he has abstracted the flowers to a formation of decorative squares hanging in an arrangement of thin vertical lines with a black space beyond.

These elegant packs did not survive the Revolution and subsequent Chinese packs have all the hallmarks of Social Realism, brawny tractor drivers, tanks in bushes and the like.

Japanese Packs

Included with these Chinese packs are two striking Japanese packs of the period, produced by the Japanese tobacco monopoly, *Air Ship* (1936) and *Hikari* (about 1935). The *Air Ship* pack is in the naturalistic tradition of the Western designer, showing an aerial ballet of modern technology – flying dangerously near to each other are aeroplanes and air ships, set against a frozen mountain range and the clear blue sky. So desperately has the designer wanted to include as many aircraft as possible that the scene has become something Surreal, worthy of Magritte's icy landscapes with apparitions in the sky. The lettering, too, seems an attempt at Western design forms, the watch-spring 'S', the dominating forms of the first letters of the brand name, the single line crossing both 'T's. But in the construction of the capital 'A' is revealed a definitely Japanese architectural form, with the three horizontal bars turning the shape into an ornamental gateway.

The other Japanese pack, *Hikari*, is more within the bounds of traditional Japanese design, and, of all the packs illustrated in this book, makes the most efficient use of a limited range of colours. The chief influence on the pack is of course Japanese prints, the mass produced images from wooden blocks, of consummate artistry yet often intended as mere pin-ups, images of actors and geishas. Also produced were perceptive and decorative visions of the natural world, flowers, water and mountains. The *Hikari* brand features a thin rim of landscape over which bursts the huge ball of the setting sun. The sharp radiating lines of the sun are interrupted only by three crucially placed clouds in the sky. With the pack opened, the sun is central, when made up, the motif is set off-centre. The high traditions of Japanese design are continued with the *Cherry* packs shown on pages 114–115.

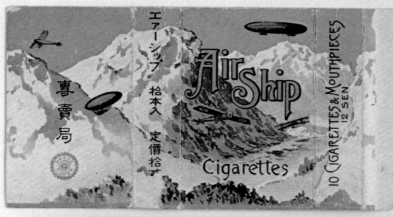

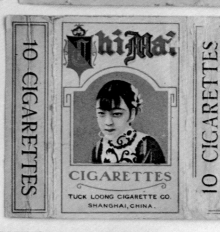

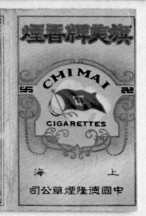

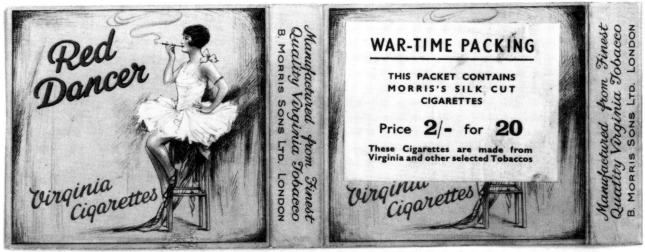

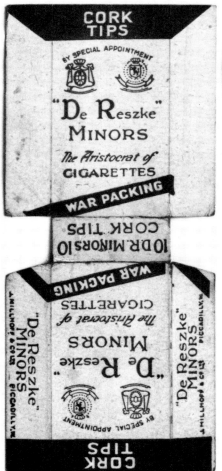

The Second World War

As in the First World War, the very conditions of total war prevented any significant use of the cigarette pack in Britain as a propaganda device. The fact that, despite the blockade, cigarettes continued to be available was perhaps propaganda enough. Economic disruption affected both the product and its packaging. On the outbreak of war the Board of Trade set up a department run by a Tobacco Controller, who fixed ration levels to the retailers. It was not until 1950 that the

Queen Wilhemina's birthday in 1941.

Packaging itself first recognized the existence of the war with special labels like that stuck on the back of the Morris' *Red Dancer* pack which announced that the cigarette was made from 'Virginia and other selected Tobaccos'. The high quality board usually used in pack production had to be abandoned. Poor quality card was used in such packs as the *De Reszke Minor*. The range of colours for printing was again drastically reduced. Ultimately, cheap board was abandoned for the paper cup. Shown here is the paper cup for Player's *Navy Cut*. It was cordially disliked by the British smoker who missed his hull-and-slide. Judging by

But recently it has been suggested by one of the original design team that there was another reason. The American Tobacco Company found that women strongly objected to the original green colour as being too masculine, and a white pack was considered more suitable for customers of both sexes. It is said that patriotism and colour psychology resulted in an increase of sales of over 30%.

In occupied countries such as Czechoslovakia and Poland, existing packs were overprinted, and as far as possible, the name of the country expunged. The *Letka* brand on cheap board shows this alteration, the stamp of Czech State Tobacco Monopoly

Government ceased controls over leaf leaving the bonded warehouses. The British smoker had, since the 1880s, preferred a straight Virginia tobacco, but dwindling supplies meant that this had to be blended with 2% exotic, mainly Turkish tobaccos. It was not until 1960 that the word Virginia re-appeared on the back of the Player's *Navy Cut* pack.

Cigarette smokers on the Continent suffered worse privations than mere rationing. In 1941 Dutch people were smoking cigars made from beetroot pulp. It was a considerable propaganda coup when the British Royal Air Force dropped packets of *Ardath* by parachute on occupied Holland to mark

the Japanese pack of 1942, war privations did not affect packaging there in quite the same way.

Advertising was curtailed both in Britain and in America, (where Roosevelt had classed the cultivation of tobacco as an essential crop for a nation at war). One of the first manifestations of the war economy on the world of packaging was the 1942 change experienced by the *Lucky Strike* pack. The gold circle was abandoned, as the copper powder in the ink base was needed for the war effort, as was the chromium base for the green ink used to print that familiar pack. The company announced that 'Lucky Strike Green has gone to War'.

(Tabakova Regie) originally read CTR. In the example shown here the 'C' of Czechoslovakia has been struck from the device, leaving plain TR. By the time the overprinted *Egypt* pack was issued, this stamp had been redesigned to fill the gap left by the missing 'C'.

There were more specific references on European cigarette packs to the Nazi occupation. There is a brand called *Baltica* which reproduces for the consumer a map of Hitler's conquests and the new designation of the conquered territories.

These grim packs come as close to Britain as the Channel Islands where, until the liberation, you could buy *Aromatica*.

America after the War

It was not until the 1950s that cigarette supplies returned to normal after the war. The American cigarette industry survived better than its European counterpart, so much so that cartons of American brands were for several years after 1945 the only stable currency until economies revived, as well as a powerful influence on European smoking habits.

Approaches to the promotion of cigarettes within the USA were increasingly affected by the new preoccupations with smoking and health, culminating in the first major governmental report, 'Smoking and Health' of 1964. Concern was sufficient by the mid 1950s to encourage a sudden growth of filter tipped brands.

Quite a number of other problems arose with the opportunities provided by the new medium of television advertising. It was all very well looking at a pack of *Old Gold* with legs on a poster, it was another thing to have them leaping around in your living room. In 1948 *Camel* sponsored the 'Camel News Caravan' and two years later the 'Lucky Strike Theatre' was started.

The main filter cigarettes of the 1950s were *Kent* (introduced 1952), *Winston* (1954), *Marlboro* filtered (1954) and *L&M* (1953). The filter tip grew logically from the old devices such as the cork mouthpieces that also compressed the end of the cigarette, the sliced cane holder, the cardboard tube, or the folded paper wadding of Brown & Williamson's *Viceroy* (1938). In 1954, *Viceroy* changed to the cellulose acetate tip, the first in a long series of complicated filter constructions that culminate in the *Doral* recessed filter (1973, see page 108).

If filters were increasingly popular then so were menthol cigarettes, *Salem* (1956) and *Newport* (1957). It is important to see these developments in the context of the increasing evidence presented to the public concerning the links between smoking and serious illnesses, and the strenuous and expensive rebuttals of the industry. As we shall see in the chapter on the modern pack, pack design and cigarette advertising changed more from 1960 to 1970 than at any time before in the history of the tobacco industry. Can we see the antecedents of the Universal cigarette in the 1950s? Certain devices did persist, for example the endorsement of the product by film stars and sportsmen. *Chesterfield* featured 'The Kings of Sport'. The design of these advertisements still showed that pleasure at packing every square inch of valuable newspaper and periodical space with information and entertainment. Typical of the post-war style is a *Chesterfield* advertisement from the 'New Yorker' in 1949. The film star, John Lund, starring in 'Brides of Vengeance' is seen elegantly puffing in front of the shelves of his library. The slogan 'ABC' floats over his head while a cigarette pack crawls up his shoulder. Beneath you will see probably the last starring role enjoyed by the famous decorative Ribbon. As if this weren't enough, up pops James M Darden, prominent tobacco farmer, of Farmville, North Carolina, appearing out of Mr Lund's sleeve.

Other conventional packs are shown, the shining, healthy pin-up of *Virginia* (1953), the *Stevenson for President* pack promoting the beaming candidate, from a specially personalized pack. From *Your Name Cigarettes* of Chicago came personalized packs for the Wilbur Burial Vault Co, the Stump Sock Co, Protecto Toilet Seat Covers, and even the 62nd Armour Dry Sausage Round Up.

While little changed the design of advertisements or the range of more unusual cigarettes, in the world of pack design something was changing.

American Successes of the Fifties

It could be argued that the best package is that which reflects in design, proportions and materials, the nature of the product inside.

Turkish cigarettes like *Murad* reflected the origin of the tobacco in the exotic subject matter, but also put across the rich, heady flavour with strong, even brilliant, opaque colours and maximum colour contrasts. Similarly menthol brands such as *Kool* (1933 Brown & Williamson) and *Penguin* (page 94) show suitably Arctic creatures stumbling about in the ice, treated in clear, transparent, often chilly colours. The more aggressively advertised brands of the 1930s had visually immediate pack fronts.

With the onset of public nervousness about smoking and health, filter cigarettes, then, came to dominate the market, and the successful brands seem to be those that adapted their designs to a low profile. Specific references in the promotion of cigarettes might strengthen one section of the market but at the cost of alienating another. In trying not to offend, slogans tended to become muted. 'Winston tastes good like a good cigarette should' may be catchy but it lacks the punch of 'Parrot cigarettes – they speak for themselves.' With the international trade increasingly important, you could carry few of the old racial and nationalist stereotypes about on your pack for fear of embarrassment. Even the brand names had to be calculated not to offend in different languages and cultures. In Belgium there is a brand called *John Thomas* that would probably not succeed very well in DH Lawrence's Nottinghamshire. And having spent ten years of my life in North London, I would not trust *Watford Egyptian Cigarettes.*

The filter revolution began really with the success of Lorillard's *Kent* in 1952. Two years later Reynolds replied with *Winston*, which by 1956 was the leading filter brand, and ten years later, America's leading cigarette. Reynolds brought out *Salem* in 1956, the first tipped menthol cigarette. Lorillard responded with *Newport* in 1957.

Yet not even the most devoted collector would claim a great distinction for these packs. *Winston* is said to have owed much of its success to the classic qualities of the pack, essentially red and white with the simplest possible banding and lettering. The design was so successful that it appears to have been used again by Reynolds for *Salem* with a frigid blue-green in place of the dynamic red. The *Newport* pack also announces its menthol chill in blues, allowing itself an eccentric, even Surreal shape somewhere between a boomerang and a stylized wave.

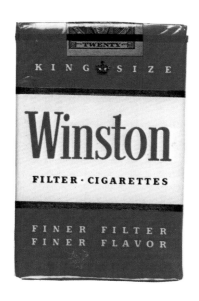

Britain after the War

The British cigarette industry was slower to recover from the war than its American counterpart, but developments in pack design took many of the same directions. Both markets were experiencing the pressures of the smoking and health issues, the switch to the filter and the emergence of the king-size. In packaging, the last remnants of the ribbons, landscapes and funny letters were swept away or, in the designer's parlance, tidied up.

Here are some examples of tidying up. The new *Woodbine* hinged lid pack retains a rich green colour but only in the vertical band on which is pinned the withered remains of that once noble plant. Above, on the lid, the Wills' Star trademark has dimly appeared, replacing the maker's name on the panel at the base of the old pack (page 48). Instead of the rising ribbons carrying the brand name, an aggressive red stripe crosses the pack horizontally. *Woodbine* is no longer 'Wild', you'll notice. Much of the change has come about because of the introduction of the hinged lid pack. As the lid is flicked back, the maker's name has to remain visible, and not just appear upside down to the person opposite.

As with Reynolds' *Salem* and *Winston* there was an attempt with Wills' *Woodbine* and *Capstan* (and also their *Bristol* brand) to establish a family resemblance between the separate brands within a company, while still permitting sufficient individuality. Wills also brought in the vertical, wrap around stripe for the new *Capstan* design. The burly form of the capstan itself, has been changed to a phantom outline on the lid. The old *Capstan* pack was a well balanced series of rectangles with plain, readable lettering. For pack identification in the 1960s all that is needed is the brand name, the symbol, and the stripe. In both *Woodbine* and *Capstan* identification is helped by the light ground, against which the letters are easily read.

Player's Navy Cut

Probably the most famous pack change of the 1950s was the loss of the Player's *Navy Cut* seascape pack. After the war, Player's had taken the opportunity of tidying up the old lettering when normal packs superseded the austerity paper cups. The long, decorated Edwardian 'C' was the first to go in March 1950, followed by other slight

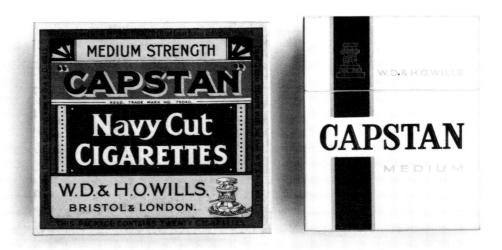

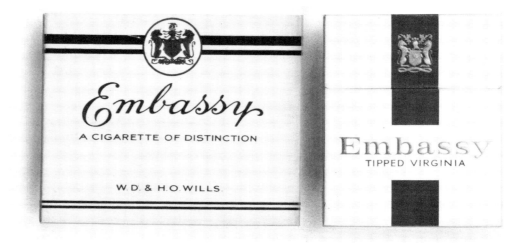

changes to improve the readability of the lettering.

On the 60th Birthday of Player's *Navy Cut* a 'Jubilee' design was produced that ran concurrently with the seascape. It showed merely the Hero trademark set against a dark blue band. The public were then asked which pack they preferred, and in March 1962 the famous *Hero* seascape was discontinued. The design that superseded featured an even smaller lifebelt; the blue stripe was edged with gold for a better looking finish. It was about this

time that Player's introduced a hinged lid pack for its *Navy Cut* but it had to be abandoned as the public in Britain preferred the hull-and-slide. As with the revised *Woodbine* and *Capstan* designs the emphasis is now firmly on the brand name. Whereas information as to the number of cigarettes held in the old pack was not allowed to interfere with the seascape, the modern *Navy Cut* pack states this clearly on the front. The success of these pack changes encouraged similar modifications in other brands such as Player's *Weights*.

Wills' Embassy

It would be unfair to call *Embassy* a revised brand. Wills had been selling an *Embassy* brand since 1914. From 1936, this pack, 'Embassy – a cigarette of great distinction' had been printed in elegant blue letters in a spacious hand-written style. The design was, above all, horizontal with repeating pairs of lines top and bottom. As a cigarette it didn't sell particularly well and it was therefore discontinued in 1959.

In August 1961 the board of Imperial approved the launch of a new coupon brand. To give the cigarette a more stylish feel than its rivals, such as *Kensitas*, it was given the name *Embassy* and, to a blaze of publicity, it was introduced in 1962. It was the British marketing success of the decade, and by 1965 it held 18.4% of the British market. Whereas other coupon brands promoted the gifts you could get, *Embassy* advertisements stressed the cigarette itself. This tone was carried over into pack itself.

The change from the personalized, specific quality of pack design before 1960 to the mass produced generalized styles after 1960 is probably nowhere better illustrated than in this comparison of *Embassy* packs pre-war and post-war. The new pack bears the characteristic Wills' family features, the vertical stripe, here coloured a brilliant and penetrating red, with the prominently placed brand name. As in all of Wills' stripe packs, the vertical stress of the front design serves to give the illusion to the smoker that he or she has a larger cigarette. The red stripe twists over the top and bottom of the pack, hence encouraging product identification when stacked in the tobacconist's shop. Probably the most important element of the design was that, although it was definitely stylish and strong, it appealed to both men and women.

Carreras' Guards

If all these brands, *Woodbine*, *Weights*, Player's *Navy Cut*, had to work from existing designs, what of the new brands that could start from scratch? Carreras' *Guards* was launched in 1960 and was probably the most influential British pack of any shown on these pages devoted to the Stripe. The design has a red panel and black square on a crisp white ground. The lettering also emphasizes this vertical stress. It is a classically simple design with beautifully disposed elements. Only the imposing figure of the Guard, the height of military chic, adds a specific reference to class or masculinity. The associations were further heightened when Carreras promoted the Guard to officer shortly after the launch.

Many of the new brands of the 1960s such as *Gold Leaf* (1960) and Player's *No 6* (1965) have been subsequently criticized for their blandness of design, and an automatic recourse to the stripe. But it has to be remembered that these simplifications would not have been adopted without public consent. It was the Public who got rid of Hero's seascape.

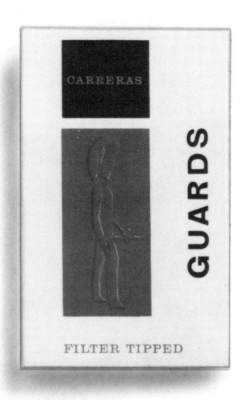

King-size and Tip Art

The career of *Pall Mall* is probably one of the most eventful in an industry where major changes are generally feared. *Pall Mall* was the first king-size cigarette, and its market success caused a radical re-alignment of forces, breaking the Big Brand hold on the market, so that, by 1959, the six largest manufacturers in the US offered twenty-seven brands in forty-four sizes and packings.

Pall Mall was originally sold as a Turkish cigarette by Butler-Butler, until the company was bought by the American Tobacco Company in 1907. By 1916 the advertising expertise of GW Hill had made them Turkish brand leaders. In 1924 they appeared in a standard size, 'It's the only smoke for your Luxury Hour . . .' at 30 cents for 20, and 5 cents more west of the Rockies. 'Take the famous red box home with you tonight and after your coffee, when you've snuggled down in your easy chair to read, relax or chat – light up a

real Pall Mall'. In 1936 domestic tobaccos were added. In 1939 the company added about 15mm to the cigarette – the King-size – and the results were so satisfactory from a sales point of view that word got around. In 1940 *Herbert Tareyton* went what it called 'modern size'.

Comparing the original *Pall Mall* box with the king-size pack, the translation is from the horizontal to the vertical. The box, with its vast expanse of red, suggested ranks of cigarettes lying within. One of the original packagings was the 'Banquet size' with crown, dedicated to 'HIM' (His Imperial Majesty the American Gentleman). This accessory to fine and cultivated living becomes the flexible, cheaper, more efficient paper cup, and, in the process, the lettering of the brand name has been drawn out like rubber bands. Even the serifs find a way to create a vertical line. Everything conspires to persuade the eye of the extreme length of the product inside. Other brands such as *Herbert Tareyton* show similar attenuation (see pages 104–105, for the *Embassy* stripe).

Having already noticed that other

development of smoking in the 1950s, the filter tip, this chapter should end with some mention of the exciting and extraordinary opportunities offered to the designer by the delights of tip technology. On packs and advertisements the artist had often been at a loss as to how to find some visual equivalent for such a simple affair as tobacco leaves smouldering in a paper tube. The copywriter had all the advantages, hinting at secret processes, eulogizing the various blends used, evoking the early days of the Tobacco Trade.

With the emergence of the filter tip, the artist could at last get to grips with a technology seemingly only rivalled in richness of imagery by the hardware of Space exploration.

The cult of tip technology probably began with *Herbert Tareyton's* Dual Filter, a pure white outer filter, combined with an inner filter of activated charcoal illustrated like some nuclear power plant on the pack.

The only British rival in ingenuity was the *Four Square* filter on Dobie's *Four Square* packs of the 1950s, showing an inner core wrapped in what appears to be several layers of old carpet.

CHAPTER NINE

CLASSIC PACKS 2

More Classic Packs – including *Gitanes* and *Gauloises* from France, *Cherry* from Japan, *Miss Blanche* from Holland and *Passing Clouds* from Britain. The more ornate and exotic Classics are represented by the yellow abstract decorations of the British Gold Flake family, and the rich sensuous absurdity of *Murad,* one of North America's best known Turkish cigarettes.

Gitanes and other French Cigarette Packs

Tobacco, it is said, first reached France as a cure for Catherine de Medici's migraine, sent by the French Ambassador to Portugal, Jean Nicot. This celebrated, if medically dubious, act of mercy was rewarded with the coining of the word Nicotine. In the seventeenth century the French government established a State Monopoly. Its powers were extended by Napoleon, who regulated the growing, curing and sale of tobacco.

A State Monopoly does tend to inhibit the proliferation of packaging, novelties and gimmicks. The insatiable hunger for new competitive images just does not seem to exist. Local illicit brands such as the famous *Sales Gueules* (literally 'Dirty Gobs', but also a highly insulting term of abuse) may have sprung up but they did not survive for long.

For most people French cigarettes mean just two brands. *Gauloises*, in the soft pack, is very much the cigarette of the people, while *Gitanes*, in all manner of decorated boxes and hull-and-slides, is definitely an up-market brand. The pack designs reinforce this distinction. Gauloises has the simple motif of a Gallic war helmet printed a darker blue on a light blue ground. With its martial and patriotic overtones, it is no surprize that the basic design was introduced just before the First World War. Less well-known is *Celtique* seen here on a poster by the influential Art Deco designer, Cassandre.

Gitanes (Gypsies) is strictly a family name for a range of cigarettes. The *Caporal* pack, launched in the early 1930s taken from a design by the well known artist M Ponty, won many prizes before 1939 in international packaging exhibitions. It shows a Gypsy girl, glimpsed through a haze of Art Deco smoke, performing a frenzied dance with tambourine on the slanted bank of lettering. *Gitanes Grammont* (about 1960) shows her on television watched by a harlequin, while in *Gitanes Caporal Superieure*, the dance is over – her tambourine and fan lie in a still-life group on a table. The pack can be seen beside the gypsy in Dransy's *Gitanes* poster of 1931.

Even the consciously more sober *Gitanes Vizir* features the gypsy; she makes a subdued appearance in a cameo. In a 1929 advertisement *Vizir* sold as 'A blend of the best Oriental tobaccos,' with the copy, 'The smoke rises, the perfume stays . . . simple but chic, without gold tips, restrained in design and packaging.' True to its words the *Vizir* pack shows the gypsy harnessed, reduced to a charming, almost Napoleonic silhouette. Splendid though it is, the *Gitanes* pack must surrender to the Algerian, *Les Deliceuses* (about 1935), for sheer enery and primitive vigour.

LES GITANES
CIGARETTES DE LA RÉGIE FRANÇAISE

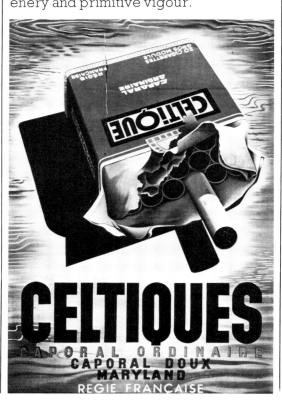

CELTIQUES
CAPORAL ORDINAIRE
CAPORAL DOUX
MARYLAND
RÉGIE FRANÇAISE

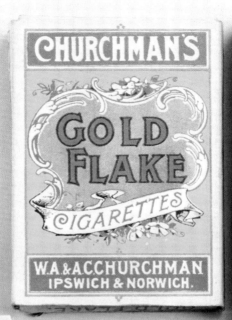

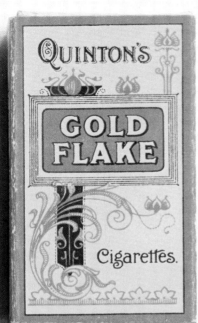

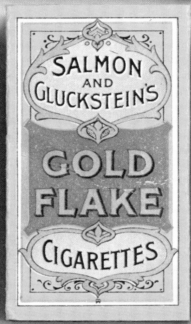

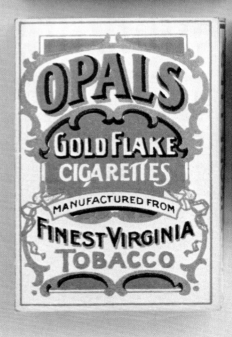

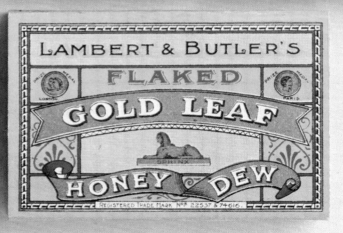

The Gold Flake Family

Unlike terms such as 'Navy Cut', which refers to the sailor's tobacco left to mature in tightly bound rolls, 'Gold Flake' is poetic rather than technical. The phrase evokes the supposed Golden glow of the cured flaked leaf ready for smoking. There is no special blend or arrangement. Yet in pack design there is a strong family resemblance

We can take Lambert & Butler's their own. The twin ribbons do their very best to help just four words, 'Gold Leaf' and the secondary brand name 'Honey Dew' to occupy vast areas of space.

Hignett's brand shares the same promise of nectar, set in the same rich colour harmonies of a dominant heavy yellow interspersed with areas of red. The avoidance of figurative imagery has again left the pack artist with the unenviable task of filling the maximum with the minimum. He has taken the bold course of dispensing with all decoration beyond panel edges, relying on the bold no-nonsense type-

Early British style, does a whiff of sulphur disturb the atmosphere.

Baker's *King Bruce* (10 with mouth-pieces) is unusual in the Gold Flake family for displaying on the front a brand character, the monarch seen with axe, framed in thistles. Here we see the exuberant back that makes up for the sober front, the rich vocabulary of form, the cartouche that becomes a ribbon, the posturing feet of the letters, the 'F' and 'K' that wave to each other. The dense yellow ground is heightened subtly with a small touch of dark green.

The association of yellow with Gold Flake seems to be universal; even in the

Flaked Gold Leaf as being typical. Shown here is a packet of 10 cigarettes with the design using a horizontal rather than a vertical stress. The Lambert & Butler pack has an almost Japanese spareness of structure and proportion, thin dowels dividing up the compartments behind for medals, lettering and an almost stencilled type of decoration. The typography is solid, and, like the proportion of the pack, stressed horizontally – the letters of 'Flaked' stretch out in a desperate effort to fill the large panel they have been allotted. In the spacing of the maker's name the 'B' and the 'S' of Butler's seem to want to walk off on

face to see him through.

Neither Quinton's *Gold Flake* nor Salmon & Gluckstein's use any recognizable brand feature or natural decoration. Quinton's prefer asymmetry with almost a hint of Art Nouveau in lily shapes and tendrils, but the solid panel and black column root the design firmly in the sensible. Salmon & Gluckstein add a breezy light blue to the standard Gold Flake palette, plaques that almost become mirrors. Both use that sensible chunky British style of lettering for the 'Gold Flake' – stable serifs, letters in low relief. Only in Quinton's 'Q' and the cigarettes' 'g' and the crossed 't's, the hallmark of the

Churchman's pack the yellow seems to have a good chance in its battle with the red. Hence it is all the more surprising and unnerving to see such a dense red flare on the pack of Opal's *Gold Flake*.

The epitome of the Gold Flake packet is Bacon's *Gold Flake* box label for 100 cigarettes. It is an astonishingly confident performance, designed in about 1920 by Mr Aronowitz, the manager of the Cambridge tobacconists, Bacon's. It has great sensitivity of touch, a pale yellow ground framed by thin red lines that decorate the central lozenge, and fill in the firm's coat-of-arms. It is shown with another, but better known label, that for Wills' *Gold Flake*.

Japan's Cherry Brand

As you would expect from a culture with such an awareness of formal relationships in the day-to-day environment, Japanese packs have generally shown the very highest standards of design. We have already seen the two separate strands of influence at work on the *Air Ship* and *Hikari* (page 101). The *Glory* pack (page 90), issued in 1928 to commemorate the coronation of the Emperor Hirohito, is typical of many in using the bold and decorative designs more usually associated with the Japanese print. The *Glory* design uses all four faces of the structure, continuing the red and white rays of the sun round the entire body of the pack. This ingenuity of thinking of all sides of the pack as a single visual unit is a quality rarely found in the Western packs.

The story of 'Buck' Duke's sortie into the Japanese market is told briefly on page 100. The ultimate failure to establish an American cigarette power in the land cannot be blamed entirely on the creation of the Japanese Tobacco Monopoly. Active opposition came from local firms who resented Duke's raucous street bands and sandwich men spelling out 'Pin Head' on Kyoto streets. But Duke under-estimated

the taste for mouthpiece cigarettes, that is cigarettes held either in small cardboard tubes or gripped in slightly conical holders. In spite of market indications Duke persisted with open-ended cigarettes, and his competitors were beginning to catch up by 1910.

The Japanese Tobacco Monopoly standardized and systematized the industry, which, by the First World War, had grown to massive proportions. The *Cherry* brand, still on sale today, was introduced in the mid 1930s. Unlike the French and Italian monopolies, the Japanese Tobacco Corporation, as the monopoly is now called, has a long tradition of issuing one brand in a series of different designs.

The earliest Cherry pack shown here dates from 1935 (10 magnum sized cigarettes) and is, incidentally, the only pack seen so far which directly features the Cherry blossom itself. The brand name *Cherry* has particular associations for the Japanese people with the coming of spring, festivals and celebrations. In Japanese and Chinese art the depiction of flowers arouses complex feelings to do with seasonal changes and renewal, and, since the tobacco industry worldwide likes to relate itself to the natural world, flowers were also convenient for the inclusion in pack designs. Nobody would pretend that the 1935 pack is outstanding – an unfortunate mixture

of Japan and Tartan, with free-floating Westernized lettering clumsily arranged. The 1936 pack reproduced with it shows considerable advances in typography. The design, which extends around the pack, makes even the pompous architectural forms beyond the trees look exciting, using a careful and refined silhouette style. What Western commercial artist would have attempted that subtle perspective that makes the building appear like some great battleship at sea. The mixed tones of light blues with stylized clouds, set against dull red, are again consistent with the more sober, teasing character of the pack. In 1900, Duke's agent observed that the Japanese avoided excess and sought mildness in smoking and eating. The same may well be said for their taste in pack design.

At a time when Western manufacturers are shying away from figures and scenes on packs, it is interesting to see the *Cherry* packs series illustrating, often photographically, a wide range of subjects almost in the cigarette card tradition, for example landscape views, sports, plants, and animals. Illustrated opposite is a selection of packs from 1974–6, some reproducing examples of traditional imagery. The *Smokin' Clean* pack, incidentally, got its name, not from its low tar content, but from attempts to stop packs from being thrown into the street.

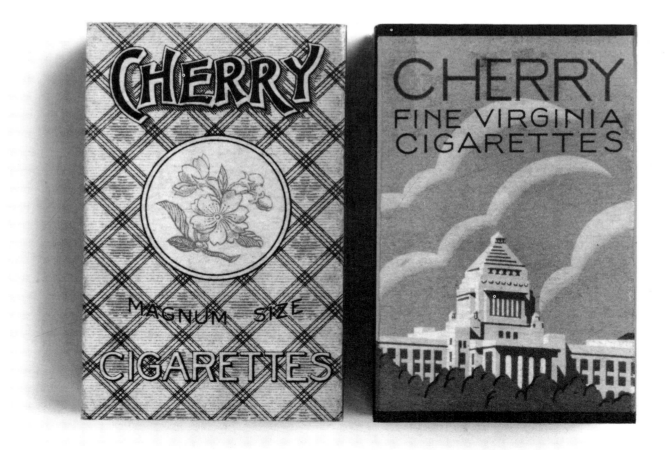

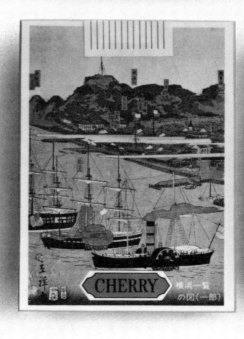

Lorillard's Murad

Lorillard, arguably America's oldest tobacco firm, was later than most companies to capitalize on the change to cigarettes from other tobacco products. Before 1900 the company, operating from the factory in Jersey City, specialized in plug tobacco, with such brands as *Golden Turtle*, *Red Cross* and *Climax*, all bonded with the company's distinctive tin disc, guaranteeing the genuine article. Lorillard was absorbed by Duke's Trust in the mid 1890s. When the Trust was dissolved in 1911, Lorillard, with Pierre Lorillard as chairman, found itself with a considerable volume of navy cut and fine-cut chewing tobacco, but also with the cigarette brands of the firm of Anargyros, New York. Anargyros had

launched such well known brands of exotics as *Egyptian Deities* and *Turkish Trophies* (both in 1891), *Turkey Red* and *Helmar* (both in 1900) and *Mogul* in 1904. By 1903 Turkish cigarettes had taken 25% of the American cigarette market. American Tobacco's exotics during this period were *Fatima* and *Mecca*. Upmarket was their *Omar*, launched in 1910. In the range of Turkish brands, probably most memorable from a visual point of view was *Murad*, begun in 1900 by Anargyros and acquired by Lorillard's in 1911.

The Turkish taste was ultimately to yield to the American Blend, such as *Camel*, and *Lucky Strike*, but it did inspire many bizarre creations in the way of the exotic pack: the straggling caravan of *Oasis* (1913, Liggett & Myers), the sultry *Turkey Red*, the baleful face of *Zira* (1910, Lorillard) and the pale, pensive face of the Poet moved by the Muse, *Omar*. Notice too, the

cluttered ornament of *Egyptian Heroes* (1915 Krinsky).

Special attention must be drawn to Melachrino's *Crocodile* 1923, a delightful design showing the beast basking on the banks of the Nile within sight of the Pyramids. Of all the animal packs this shows a particularly unlikely anatomical construction.

The *Murad* box has all the sheer visual brilliance and ultimate absurdity of Griffith's Biblical epics with grandiose scale, hilarious ornament, and smouldering passion.

The design for the back of the box is reproduced in the Introduction, together with the source for the construction of the two stumpy pillars.

It is perhaps typical of this age of wicked pack humour, that the brand was named after the Emperor Murad IV of Turkey, who banned the smoking of tobacco, and executed those who disobeyed.

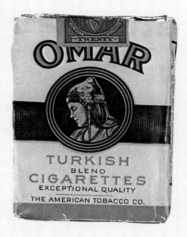

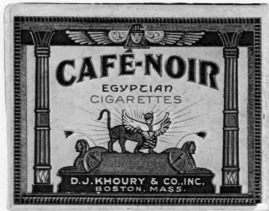

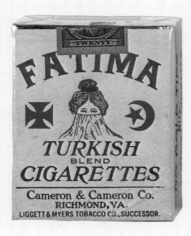

MISS BLANCHE
GOLD LEAF
VIRGINIA

Miss Blanche
VIRGINIA
CIGARETTES
MAGNUMS
THE VITTORIA EG. CIG. CO.

HIGH CLASS
VIRGINIA

Miss Blanche
WHITE LABEL

25

Miss Blanche
EXTRA MILD CIGARETTES

BAT's Miss Blanche

Miss Blanche is a well-established brand of cigarettes made initially by the Vittoria Cigarette Company of Rotterdam, which in 1935 was purchased by the British-American Tobacco Company. As well as continuing to sell in Holland, it was exported widely, particularly to Siam, whose smokers had a penchant for pin-up packs. Over the years, the demands of fashion have dictated that Miss Blanche herself has gone through more transitions than any other brand character.

Of all the major European ladies who star on the packs, no-one seems to relish a cigarette more than Miss Blanche, no-one keeps the thing so close to the lips, ready for instant enjoyment. Yet she is not so self-centred as to exclude us, the customers, from her gaze. Her enthusiasm has to be unquestioned because she is selling one of the most difficult of commodities, the cigarette for women.

The brand name covers a wide range, the Egyptian cigarette, the American (flanked by the Stars and Stripes), large, medium and small, in plain, tipped and assorted colours. Some are given suitably exotic names, the *Golden Slipper*, the *Favorite*. The *Gold Leaf Virginia* pack, of about 1930, shows Miss Blanche at her most innocent, seemingly oblivious of the column of smoke rising vertically past her eyes. The boyish grin is gone in the *Virginia Magnums* pack, the cigarette held archly to the lips, while her eyes smoulder under the rim of her hard hat. This representation shows her at her most mannish, perhaps with associations of the Hunting Pink, the riding crop and hat. Her manifestation after 1950 in the Extra Mild pack clarifies the hunting theme, but the look is glossy and antiseptic. Perhaps her most stunning appearance is on this pre-war *Favorite* pack, swathed in an evening dress of silk, with an extrovert feathery turban. In all her packs she displays an independence and self-assertion rare on packs featuring women.

The image of a woman carrying a lit cigarette on packs is not common; on many packs women appear to be passively waiting for the desired flame. Even today, despite gestures towards sexual equality, advertisements for women's cigarettes have tended to deny the woman independent, un-interrupted smoking. All too often women's cigarettes have been sold as objects with which to entice men; the request for a light being an ideal excuse for contact between strangers.

Attitudes have changed however. In 1901 'Ladies' Realm' asked well-known ladies, 'Should women smoke?' 'Of course they should if they like it,' said Princess Gagarine. Evelyn Lang found the lady smoker, 'a horrid unfeminine creature. In a more positive vein Mrs Hugh Fraser advised all ladies to 'learn how to do it without making an exhibition of yourself; don't make faces; don't inhale and avoid cheap cigarettes.' Before the First World War only the bohemienne among ladies smoked whenever she liked. Ladies usually smoked Egyptian or Turkish cigarettes in private, among friends or at the toilet table. It was said that, so enraged was a waiter at a fashionable hotel to see a lady smoking in public, he smacked her face and knocked her over. Ironically, women's cigarettes are now one of the few areas of growth in the tobacco industry.

THE VITTORIA EGYPTIAN CIGARETTE Cº

CIGARETTE SPECIALISTS

Miss Blanche

FAVORITE

MIDDLE SIZE

Player's Passing Clouds

Passing Clouds was Player's major Class C cigarette, made from expensive high grade tobaccos, and produced by the company for prestige rather than financial viability. The brand was on sale from 1874 to 1973 and was famous for the oval shape of the cigarette and its pink pack.

The image of the Cavalier smoking is of course an anachronism – cigarettes were a nineteenth-century invention as far as Britain was concerned. It has been suggested that we could be looking at a modern Toff about to go off to a fancy dress ball. Both image and brand name are central to the major psychological reasons for smoking. The Cavalier, so familiar from seventeenth-century Dutch portraiture, tended to have that swashbuckling, hedonistic attitude to life that cigarette manufacturers would like us to adopt. The brand name at once suggests that depression is momentary and can be dispelled by a cigarette, (indeed every cloud has a silver lining), and reminds us of the attractions of blowing cloud patterns in the air as you smoke. The earlier

pack showed actual clouds in the sky on the reverse side, as well as the cloud exhaled by the smoker.

The design has further implications. The earlier pack, an approved proof by British-American Tobacco for export, has the Cavalier, still wearing hat and sword, seated at a table. He has left his book for a quick smoke from the open box beyond. He leans back expansively, one hand resting lazily on the arm of the chair, the other casually holding a cigarette as he puffs out a great cloud of smoke. Staring pensively into it, he muses on life and its vicissitudes. The meditative pipe smoker is a familiar subject in art. The images of clouds of smoke, or of soap bubbles blown by children's pipes, were used to suggest the fleeting nature of human life, and the vanity of man's wishes. As late as the nineteenth century, the French painter Edouard Manet was to exploit both smoke and bubbles for such ends, and the British painter, John Everett Millais' famous painting *Bubbles*, exhibited in 1886, is another exploration of the theme. Presumably neither Messrs A&F Pears (who, despite Millais' disapproval, used the painting to advertise their soap the following year) nor WD&HO Wills can have been aware of these associations when they

authorized the use of these images.

A comparison between the two packs, the export pack and the more recent hinged lid pack, reveals several interesting details of the way in which packs were modernized. First, the actual size of the panel bearing the brand character has been drastically reduced. The lettering has lost a certain amount of serif growth and the capital 'C' has been restrained from its pincer movement on the 'L'.

Interestingly, the brand name has lost its inverted commas, a pruning experienced by many British brands of the post-war years. Although this is in line with twentieth-century economies in punctuation, it does also serve to identify the brand name more closely with the product, rather than with its original meaning; *Passing Clouds* thus becomes the cigarette rather than a reference to the lifting of depression. The ultimate pruning occurred to *Passing Clouds* in 1973 when it was discontinued.

From the 1950s, and for reasons we have seen already, cigarette packs were being systematically put through the process of 'tidying up'. Brand characters shrank, it was the dawning of the Age of the Stripe, the birth of the Universal cigarette.

CHAPTER TEN

MODERN PACK ART

Since the 1950s packs have become more simple and restrained, forsaking the florid and narrative for the visually more immediate stripe. Older types of pack are being superceded by the more chic lines of the hinged lid pack, with its glossy laminated surfaces, returning to the sophisticated sheen and design of the old hand-filled Cigarette Cases.

Pop, Op and the Minimal in the 1960s

From the 1950s there was, as we have seen, a retreat from figurative imagery on the packs, an iconophobia brought on by anxieties about pleasing a mass market. At the same time, as a reaction against cosmic concerns among American Abstract Expressionist painters, (a lead-footed earnestness that many felt constricting in subject matter and methods), American artists began to respond in an ironic, often secretly joyful way to the visual richness of advertising imagery. 'I am for Kool art, 7-Up art, Pepsi-art, Sunshine art, 39 cents art, 15 cent art, Vatronal art, Dro-Bomb art, Vam art, Menthol art, L&M art . . .', wrote Claes Oldenburg in 1961. Cigarette packs inspired many images; they were so readily available, in such a variety of forms, anonymous, insignificant and disposable. The artist was attracted by the way that non-products were sold in the most bizarre, kitschy, surreal, and complex way.

Mel Ramos painted one of his open-eyed, seductive, all American syrens beside a pack of Philip Morris, the Petty *Old Gold* pin-up stripped, polished and naked. Questions of dimension render the pack enormous or her a midget. The pack is a rock, a mute support. She is there to ease your worries, amplify your pleasures. But not all Art about Packs is so fleshy.

The Pack in Pop Art

Two artists particularly have used themes of pack figuration and structure in their art. The American painter Larry Rivers has produced a witty series of pack paintings starting with *Thin Tareyton* (1960) and *Disque Bleu* (1961). This work culminated in the ambitious *Friendship of America and France: Kennedy and De Gaulle*, where the respective leaders glower over walls of characteristic packs, *Disque Bleu* balanced by *Lucky Strike*, a *Camel* sniffing airily at a *Gitanes* pack (1961–1962). In 1962 he produced a droll series inspired by the *Camel* pack, *Camels*, *Graph Camel* and *Amel Camel* among others. The contours and modelling of the animal that have fascinated generations, are rubbed and scumbled on to the canvas, the brand name going through endless variations, 'Am' . . . 'Me' . . . 'Amel' . . . 'Mel'. In *Graph Camel* Old Joe sniffily tolerates the imposition of a grid, while, above, in a desert dream he disports himself in the sand, pursuing a two-humped near relative. That the *Camel* pack still occupies the imagination of the artist and designer can be seen from the 'Warped Vision' presented on the cover of the album, 'Mirage' (below).

The British painter Richard Smith has written of his own pack-inspired art of the 1960s, 'The kind of images I was using then were based on cartons, or boxes. The carton is an incessant theme in present day civilization: the shops are full of boxes and you see these before you see the goods; they practically stand in for the goods – it is not just a question of labelling or depiction. Everything comes in boxes: you buy boxes when you are shopping, you do not buy visible goods; you don't buy cigarettes only cartons. The box is your image of the product.'

Richard Smith's *Kent* painting was, in his own words, 'based on that specific cigarette pack, and the reference to "Kent" is in fact a reference to the filters which used to have a bluish

tinge.'

Yet it is ironic that at the same time as Pop Art was beginning to look at Packs, the Pack Artist was looking, not at the lubricious interiors of Tom Wesselmann, or at Warhol's packaging industry, but at recent developments in American minimalism.

The Stripe Style

The predominant pack style of the last twenty years has been the stripe style. Wills' typically British compromise *Regal* has its stripes on the diagonal, thinly threaded with gold and, with its crest, aspiring to the dignity of some Order of the Garter.

American stripes are flat, democratic and dynamic, an integral part of the pack, and not just superimposed on the structure. But why stripes? Again and again one is reminded of the work of the American minimalists, painters like Kenneth Noland and Frank Stella.

The stripes on the *Virginia Slims* filter pack, shades of red on a neutral yellow toned background, are slim and attenuated, as elegant as the Dior clad women (liberated but so fluffy) that sport the cigarette in advertisements. The stripes do give the illusion of elongating the cigarettes, 'Slimmer than the fat cigarettes men smoke'. In the advertisements the cigarettes seem to appear through the top of the pack on its striped side, launched as steely white missiles from the redness and heat.

Golden Lights uses the same device but accompanied by the castle trademark. A quick check through the old *Embassy* filter advertisements shows again the stripe juxtaposed with the tumescent cigarettes. Pack art in the 1960s and 1970s has seen the production of countless stripes, echelons and panels. In *Vantage's* case the pack motif is a modernized target pack with pretentions to optical fun and games.

Sherman's Premium (Gold Filter, Cigarettes in Colour, Queen Size) masses two perfect rainbow dispositions of colour arches, more a colour exercise than, as they would have been in the past, a symbolic exercise in rendering Hope. The *Merit* pack uses a sort of symmetry, two opposing diagonals resolved with a joint area that settles the central zone into a virtual square, where the Philip Morris coat of arms can live.

If packs have to project character and identity, have to have something that the smoker is not ashamed of being seen with, why did American designers come to rely so heavily on stripes? Firstly, for the same reason that dictated the disappearance of the Tareyton Toff, that previous imagery has been seen as hierarchical – the society hostess, the smart set – with direct pictorial allusions to the élite. Devices such as the seemingly autographed pack, with the management's personal endorsement, revealed the essentially deceitful nature of the design – these are after all mass-produced products.

Stripes are non-hierarchical, a pure and immediate statement capable of mass production, that can be read without special knowledge or social advantage. The pack design philosophy of the late 1960s and 1970s is uncannily like that of the American minimalists, of Frank Stella's paintings in particular, 'all I want anyone to get out of my paintings . . . is that you can see the whole idea without any confusion.' What more appropriate than this utter visual immediacy of the pack, creating an identity that offends nobody, and in the process making a long cigarette look even longer?

The Universal Pack

The concern about smoking and health on both sides of the Atlantic culminated in the American Surgeon-General's Report of 1964 two years after the College of Surgeons' Report in Britain. A few years after, packs had to carry health warnings in the USA and then Britain, and then came the bans on television advertising of cigarette brands. The British Code of Advertising practice July 1977 specifies that the advertiser must not persuade people to start smoking in posters and press advertising, not persuade people to smoke more, exaggerate the attractions of smoking, exploit the vulnerable, claim it is natural to smoke,

or necessary for relaxation, is more manly or enhances female charm, feature the heroes of the young, or advertise directly to the young, and must refrain from linking the product with success in business life, sport, or sexual prowess. The cynic may claim that this litany is virtually a description of pack art before the Sixties, so how then do the packs of the last ten years respond to the new and increasing constraints?

All packs now bear the Health Warning, but it has become such a familiar part of the image that it is now generally considered to be useless as a deterrent, disregarded and very often concealed by the smoker's fingers. Swedish packs carry any one of fifteen different wordings to combat the smoker's immunity to the standard wording.

The Decorator Pack

Of more serious impact have been the constraints on imagery. The pack designer has now to produce a 'classy but classless' concept that can be used in the few contexts permitted the advertiser. One solution has been what is sometimes called the Decorator Pack, the pack made of glossy single colour card, such as the John Player *Special Filter* launched in 1971. The decorator pack has to be functional on every occasion. Whereas the bottle of washing up liquid is seen only by the few people every day who are allowed access to your kitchen, the cigarette pack is probably seen and judged by hundreds of people every day. You are the pack you produce.

What more convenient for the 1970s than an extension of 1960s minimalism to its natural conclusion, the pack as

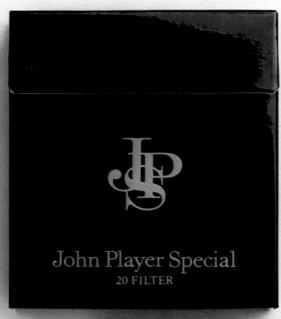

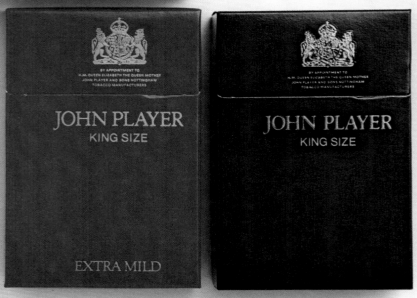

bland and stylish as the first cigarette cases. On the decorator pack, particularly popular in Britain, the stripes are gone, the gold edging banned, the great colour field reigns supreme. The brand name has disappeared, not even a number remains. John Player *King Size* is about as essential as you can get. Admittedly there is a last hint of the eighteenth-century tobacco merchant in stressing the first name 'John'. The only aesthetic variable is sheen, the surface luster of the pack as it is moved in the light, sending off expensive looking radiations.

One of the best known decorator packs is the Benson & Hedges *Special Filter*, featured some time ago in distinguished and deserted rooms, and now appearing in sub-Surreal scenes of such irrationality that no Advertising Code could object. In the last twenty years great areas of flashing gold and silver proved popular with the smoking public in Britain, Player's *Perfectos* and *Grosvenor*, and Wills' *Three Castles*. The effect is mainly achieved by laminated foil glued to carton board. At the packaging works it can be printed with a large range of transparent inks for all types of luxurious finish. The Benson & Hedges *Special Filter* uses an extra variant in the embossed coat of arms and the company device on the lid. The designer has used the very minimum of lettering to emphasize the sheer weight of gold surface reflecting the light, the very epitome of 'Classy but Classless'.

This tendency to reduce specific imagery, to appeal to generalized emotions, the retreat from the individual to the mass, can be seen throughout the cigarette brands of the 1970s. Packs and advertisements have, to quote Jeremy Bugler, to be 'All things to all men . . . The Universal Cigarette.'

Changes in Advertising

Further restrictions on cigarette advertising and inhibitions on consumption as printed in the Advertising Code have caused some odd changes in imagery. Vehicle sports appear in place of athletic achievement, and market researchers in Britain have discovered that the use of horses and riding in advertisements is preferred to other activities that feature smoking because most people see it as classy but classless. It can also live quite happily within the letter and spirit of the Code.

American brands tend to be not quite so reticent in pack and advertisement, perhaps because the companies have

greater resources to gamble on the introduction of new brands. A new launch after all can cost in the region of $50 million. You can get some idea of the turbulence of the market in one report published in May, 1977, noting current plans within the industry. *Kent Golden Lights 100s* were going national that month, *Kool Super Lights* in July and *Newport Lights* in the Autumn. *Real* was to come out in June. *Lark II* was testing in Florida and Philip Morris were planning a new menthol cigarette. *American Lights* were testing in San Diego and Los Angeles, and *Kent Light Deluxe 100s* were on sale in New York County. Although this activity does reflect the rush to cater for an expanding low-tar section, it also indicates the mercurial state of the market.

Positive Packs in America

It is valid to ask at this point whether the

pack has any positive contribution to make to the success of the brand. It is virtually impossible to say with any certainty. Inappropriate imagery on the general promotional campaign of which the pack is only part, can ruin chances of success. 'You're never alone with a Strand', ran the slogan in Britain. Who wants to be thought lonely in the first place? The brand failed.

Recent American pack design is generally more prominent, with greater potential for a positive contribution to marketing. A pack like Lorillard's *Zack* (1976) is certainly more obtrusive in its character than any European brand, pretending to be the very pocket that contains it. The *Maryland 100s* pack (American Tobacco Co, 1970) was, in the temper of the times, a brave attempt to return to the figurative, here a mural design of Horse and Hounds gathering for the start of the Day's

Chase. But the brand was withdrawn the very year of its launch, and it is significant that, of the leading American cigarettes, only *Camel* still has really pronounced pictorial imagery, while so many of the leading brands of the 1970s, *Marlboro*, *Salem*, *Kent* and *Chesterfield*, owe their visual identity to designs established in the 1950s.

Two recent designs however show a greater sensitivity to public pressures. *Decade* (Liggett, 1977) uses a pack front derived from Pop Art, flashy geometrical icons of numbers and letters by such painters as Robert Indiana. The 'D' stands for the decade of research it took to develop the brand. On the reverse of the pack all is made clear, 'It took ten years to develop a "Total System" capable of delivering truly satisfying taste in a low "tar" cigarette'. Of equal significance is the *Fact* pack, rather like a clipping from a newspaper, using sheer weight of copy instead of visual imagery.

The proliferation of brands has meant high visibility colours, simple shapes, subtle, insinuating associations of clarity, focus, cleanliness and, particularly in Britain, the magpie glitter of fool's gold and silver. The pack no longer shows us sportsmen, soldiers, sailors, monarchs or drunks.

But where will the pack be going next after minimalism – given the existing economic climate that still permits expensive packaging? Other consumer products in Britain have used nostalgia as a theme of their advertising and packaging. As I write, Player's have launched a poster campaign featuring the return of Hero's head behind the blue decorator pack of the John Player *King Size*. It is a chastening thought that this book in itself may eventually reflect a new direction for packaging.

PACK IDENTIFICATION INDEX

A reference list of the cigarette packs that appear in this book grouped country by country under company names.

GENERAL INDEX

Compiled by Miss J Dudley ALA